121 TIPS
FOR BETTER
BRIDGE

121 TIPS
FOR BETTER
BRIDGE

PAUL MENDELSON

EBURY
PRESS

12

First published by Stanley Paul in 1995, as *100 Tips for Better Bridge*

This revised edition published in 2010 by Ebury Press,
an imprint of Ebury Publishing

A Random House Group Company

The Random House Group Limited Reg. No. 954009

Addresses for companies within the Random House Group can be found at
www.randomhouse.co.uk

A CIP catalogue record for this book is available from the British Library

Penguin Random House is committed to a sustainable future for
our business, our readers and our planet. This book is made from
Forest Stewardship Council® certified paper.

FSC MIX Paper from responsible sources FSC® C018179 www.fsc.org

To buy books by your favourite authors and register for offers visit
www.randomhouse.co.uk

Printed and bound in Great Britain by Clays Ltd, St Ives plc

ISBN 9780091936051

CONTENTS

INTRODUCTION

The best way to learn bridge is to play with better players. Slowly, through trial and error (as well as a lecture or two, some embarrassment and, inevitably, the occasional utter humiliation), your mind begins to store the gems of knowledge vital for success in every Game you play.

121 Tips for Better Bridge is a quick, palatable, good-natured substitute for those potentially angst-ridden hours at the green baize. Unlike so many partners, it will encourage and enthuse you. Indeed, in terms of accumulating knowledge, a couple of pages of this book is equivalent to a whole session of play, probably more, because you might not experience some of these situations for months, and then face a whole series of associated problems for which you would be unprepared. The confidence generated by increased knowledge at the bridge table is worth thousands of points alone.

Many books of tips contain great ideas for situations which almost never occur. *121 Tips for Better Bridge* unashamedly deals with the commonplace – because it is those hands which will decide whether you are a winner or a loser. The idea here is to provide you with a mental boost which will stay with you as you play any style of game: social bridge, high-stake rubber bridge, or competitive duplicate pairs. All being well, at just the right moment, the right tip will come to mind and, in a split second, transform your prospects.

Many of my students can attest to the fact that, in my classes, though they may dread the appearance of set hands, the critical points they contain can stay with them for ever. The problem – they claim – is that in a prepared hand, they are expecting a 'trap' and so they are on the lookout for it. The solution is simple, however. Treat every randomly dealt hand as if it is a set hand. If you can't find the trap, maybe there isn't one. But, if you can, you'll be ready to dodge it and emerge victorious.

Over the years, I've been given, or read about, many tips from the world's great players. Here are a couple of general pointers which I think are spot-on.

Bob Hamman – for 35 years ranked the most successful tournament player in the world – has some advice for partnerships.

'I always assume,' he says, 'that whatever my partner does, however peculiar it might seem, he is correct, and I act accordingly. If it turns out that what he did was completely wrong, then I can always discuss it later or, if necessary, change my partner. But, if you don't trust your partner while you are playing, then you are both wasting your time.'

Think about all the partnerships you see huffing and puffing, sighing and eye-rolling during a hand, and you'll realise that they've lost even before they've started.

Eric Rodwell and Jeff Meckstroth have been one of the top pairs in the world Game for four decades. On winning the International Pairs in London, they told the audience their top tip.

'In defence,' Eric Rodwell said, 'approach every hand you play in the belief that the contract can be broken …

'Place your partner with the cards he needs to defeat the contract,' his illustrious partner continued seamlessly. 'You would be surprised how many hands can be beaten this way, whereas if you give up early on, you never stand a chance …'

So often, like many sports, success at bridge is about focus. The ability to define what needs to be done to win and then doing it … Getting from A to B without digressing.

Much of the information in this book will be of use to you, the individual, at the table. There are also several tips which you should share immediately with your partner, in the defence section and also in the brand new tips on Duplicate Pairs.

Perhaps the quickest way of all to improve is to keep the cards in front of you when you play a hand. Then, at the end, you and your partner or group can discuss (and I mean discuss, not bicker and bitch) how you might have improved your bidding, play or defence. It is inevitable that you were not perfect in one area. This need not become a chore. Indeed, I find the whole bridge-playing experience very dull without the chance to have seen where I went wrong. This system also prevents the inevitable 'unlucky expert' providing an uninvited discourse on how, if someone at the table had done something else, his play would have been right. With the potential for the cards to be laid out in front of you, you will find that the most opinionated and bossy players are unexpectedly silent. Until now, they have flourished on the fact that the hands have been lost for ever, and no one will dare argue with them. Like all bullies the simplest, and best, antidote is to call their bluff.

Above all, improving your Game should enhance your enjoyment of bridge. And this book is intended to help you enjoy your improvement.

Finally, I faced the recurring dilemma of whether to call the partner 'He' or 'She'. Henry Palmer, a keen player and recently retired judge, has come to my rescue with paragraph 6 of the Interpretation Act 1978, which states:

Gender and number

6. In any Act unless the contrary intention appears:
   (a) words importing the masculine gender include the feminine;
   (b) words importing the feminine gender include the masculine;
   (c) words in the singular include the plural and words in the plural include the singular.

I am certain that this makes it all entirely clear.

1 / IF THERE IS A MISFIT, IT IS FOR BOTH SIDES – AND YOU WANT TO DEFEND

This is certainly one of the most important bidding understandings there is. If one side has an eight-card fit, it is almost certain that the other will have an eight-card fit also (there is a very small possibility of three seven-card fits instead). Even more significantly, if your opponents do not hold a fit, then nor do you, and defending is the way to win.

South	N	E	S	W
♠ 8	1S	2D	2H	3C
♥ KJ8643	NB	3D	?	
♦ K42				
♣ A63				

If you are tempted to bid 3H here, think again. Your partner has opened with a suit in which you hold a singleton; your opponents are arguing after an overcall (the fact that West was prepared to suggest another minor suit at the 3-level, when you know East-West hold limited points) and this all sounds like a significant misfit. At Duplicate Pairs, you might double for penalties; at Teams or Rubber bridge, a pass is modest, but far better than bidding on.

Conversely, when one side holds a fit, you are almost certain to hold one also and you should be keen to compete aggressively.

South	N	E	S	W
♠ 8	–	–	1H	1S
♥ AQ864	NB	2S	?	
♦ K86				
♣ AJ98				

This is a clear-cut take-out double. Your opponents hold eight spades; your side will hold an eight-card fit in one of the other suits; doubling allows your partner to choose which one. If your opponents continue to 3S, leave them there. You may have done enough to push them a level too high.

South	N	E	S	W
♠ KQJ8	–	1H	Dbl	4H
♥ 4	NB	NB	?	
♦ AJ106				
♣ AQ63				

This time, East-West rate to have at least a nine-card fit, maybe more. On that basis, once again you should double. This is still for take-out. If East-West have bid to 4H on a 4-4 fit, your partner will hold four hearts and may well pass your double. Those four trumps, combined with your strength, will lead to 4H being handsomely defeated. The bigger the heart fit East-West hold, the bigger your fit will be with partner's longest suit. 4S and 5C or 5D are all still possible Games for your side.

2 / A LEAP TO GAME IN PARTNER'S SUIT IS WEAK

They play for modest stakes at TGR's 'Big Game' in London. Usually, only a meagre Chicago Game for £50 or £100. When the likes of Zia Mahmood and Bob Hamman fly in, however, the bets increase, and £200, £300 or even £500 per hundred is not unusual.

In my experience the finer the players, the better the behaviour and atmosphere at the table. When comments do fly, they are usually sent on their way with a smile or a wink. In the case of this example, however, Zia's comment was intended to carry the weight of some considerable frustration.

Dealer South	♠ A6532		*N*	*E*	*S*	*W*
N/S Game	♥ K863		–	–	1H	NB
	♦ A9		**4H**			
	♣ 105					

♠ 109	♠ J7
♥ 4	♥ 109
♦ QJ1085	♦ 7632
♣ KJ874	♣ AQ963

```
        ♠ KQ84
        ♥ AQJ752
        ♦ K4
        ♣ 2
```

At Game All, Zia, sitting South, opened 1H and, over West's pass, North – who shall remain anonymous – leapt to 4H. This was passed out, virtually without thought. Robert Sheehan, West, led Q♦, and within seconds all the hands were thrown in and 13 tricks claimed. 6H is rock solid and, without a club lead, 13 tricks were laydown.

'I don't understand you British,' Zia complained, throwing his arms into the air in exasperation. 'Everyone else in the world plays 1H-4H shows nothing. Having two Aces is impossible ...'

His fairly weighty opponents, Bob Hamman and Robert Sheehan, nodded sagely.

With strong supporting hands, you have a multitude of ways to describe your hand, from a 'Pudding Raise' to Splinters, Swiss, or Jump-Shift (see Tip 11).

When you have a weak hand with big support for your partner, you still have your opponents to worry about: they have a big fit too, and may be able to bid a Game or a Slam if you give them bidding space. To raise partner dramatically cuts out their room for manoeuvre.

The 1H-4H or 1S-4S raise is a two-edged sword: if partner is weak, you have silenced the opposition: if he is strong, thanks to your great shape, he will probably make the contract.

In Acol, the point-count for this immediate jump to Game is 0–9pts. This hand takes the principle to the extreme:

    ♠ 10865432
    ♥ –
    ♦ 9863
    ♣ 32

The best way to stop your opponents bidding 4H is to bid 4S first! Partner opens 1S, and the next hand passes. Leap to 4S immediately. If partner is strong, he'll make 10 tricks; if he is weak, your opponents will be able to make 10, 11 or even 12 tricks … but will they come in at the 5-level?

3 / A 1NT RESPONSE DOES NOT PROMISE A BALANCED HAND

This is the kind of bidding problem which crops up regularly, and one for which many books seem reluctant to suggest a solution.

South	N	S
♠ –	1S	?
♥ 972		
♦ KQ109832		
♣ J63		

The 1NT response simply tells your partner that you are not strong enough to bid at the 2-level. In Acol, this shows 6–8pts, sometimes 9pts; in other systems, you might hold up to 11pts to respond 1NT.

On this hand, a 1NT response will avoid over-exciting your partner. If he re-bids another suit, you can pass; if he re-bids 2S, you can bid 3D (showing a six- or seven-card diamond suit with less than about 8pts); if he passes, the contract will not be too bad. Utilising the 1NT response for both balanced and distributional poor hands is a vital tool in the struggle to bid accurately with a really difficult bad hand.

If you choose to respond 2D, your partner will move towards Game with a slightly better opening hand and, whatever Game he chooses, it is likely to fail.

As for distribution, the bid categorically denies a four-card major suit which you could have shown at the 1-level, and definitely does not promise a balanced hand – as you can see from the first example.

South	N	S
♠ K32	1C	1H
♥ J985		
♦ K82		
♣ J63		

It is vital to show any four-card major suit at the 1-level, rather than responding 1NT. Failure to do so may result in missing a 4-4 fit in hearts. It does not matter that the suit quality is poor. Even if you end up in NTs, bidding hearts will dissuade the opponents from leading that suit – a useful tactical measure.

In modern Acol, restrict a 1NT response to 6–8pts, and extend this to 9pts for when you have a void or singleton in the suit your partner opened. Reserve 1NT for the really bad hands where you have to bid something, but there is nothing else available.

4 / YOU MUST HOLD TWO STOPPERS IN THE OPPONENT'S SUIT TO BID NTS

Playing and defending no-trump contracts is a simple race – which side can get their long suit established and producing tricks first. If you are playing in a NT contract without sufficient high cards in the opponent's suit, this is a race you will always lose.

East		N	E
♠ A4		1S	?
♥ KQ9			
♦ KQ32			
♣ QJ62			

Do not be tempted to overcall 1NT on this hand, because unless your partner can help you in spades, your one stopper is not enough, and a NT contract will probably fail. A take-out double is the better bid here.

The reason that you need two stoppers (high cards, or length, which will stop your opponents from cashing tricks) is that you will have the first knocked out on the lead, and you will need a second to regain the lead if you lose control whilst setting up your own long suit.

However, if your long suit is already established, then one stopper will be sufficient:

East		N	E
♠ A2		1S	1NT
♥ J98			
♦ AKQJ82			
♣ J4			

Here, a 1NT overcall is a very good bid. On the likely spade lead, you have seven top tricks, ready for the taking. If your partner has the points to raise you, you will be delighted.

Notice that this bid is totally in keeping with our order of priorities: to avoid 5C and 5D as contracts and aim for 3NT.

The general rule of requiring two stoppers in the opponent's suit does not apply merely to an immediate overcall, it remains relevant throughout the auction:

North		**N**	**E**	**S**	**W**
♠ KJ86		1S	NB	2D	2H
♥ K75		?			
◆ AQ3					
♣ KQ7					

Here, North should not risk a NT re-bid with only one stopper in hearts. Instead, he should make a bid which asks for help in hearts from partner. If South holds as little as ♥Qx or ♥Jxx, this provides the second stopper. Experts might double here to ask for more information, but most players would opt to bid 3H (see Tip 6). This bid of the opponent's suit forces partner to bid no-trumps if he can help in hearts, or failing that, to describe his hand further.

5 / IF THREE SUITS HAVE BEEN BID, YOU MUST HAVE TWO STOPPERS IN THE UNBID SUIT TO BID NTS

Look at this simple auction. In which suit does South hold his *best* cards?

	N	S
	1H	1S
	2C	3NT

The answer is probably diamonds. This is because, if South is a good player, he should have two stoppers in diamonds. **You need two stoppers in this unbid suit, because it is the most likely to be led. You will use one of your stoppers to win the first trick, and another to regain the lead when you lose to an opponent whilst establishing extra tricks in your long suit.** If your partner cannot rely upon you to have two stoppers, he will never be able to judge whether to pass 3NT when you bid it, or pull it to an alternative contract.

As in the previous tip, there is an honourable exception:

South		N	S
♠ 85		1S	2D
♥ 42		2H	?
♦ AKQJ65			
♣ A76			

3NT is fine here. Despite holding only a single club stopper, the solid diamond suit means that bidding 3NT is well worth the risk. If you bid anything else, you might miss the easiest Game contract.

Without a solid source of tricks, but with a good hand, and only one stopper in the fourth suit, there is a bid to solve your problems:

South		N	S
♠ 85		1S	2D
♥ K42		2H	?
♦ AQJ65			
♣ A76			

South's correct bid here is 3C – Fourth Suit Forcing (see Tip 31). This bid strongly suggests one stopper in clubs, but not two. Partner is forced to describe his hand further, and the best contract will be reached.

So, when you are considering bidding no-trumps as a final contract remember that, unless your own suit is a solid source of tricks, you must have two stoppers in the unbid suit to bid no-trumps.

6 / IF YOU LIKE WHAT YOU'RE HEARING BUT DON'T KNOW WHAT TO SAY – BID THE OPPONENT'S SUIT

Unless you have specific bidding arrangements with your partner, it is generally understood that to bid a suit previously bid by the opponents is a means of jolting your partner awake from his customary snooze.

An immediate 'parrot bid' or cue-bid of the opponent's suit usually has a conventional meaning, often describing a two-suited hand. A bid later in the auction, below the level of 3NT, is often used as an enquiry as to whether partner has a stopper in the suit so that you can play in NTs.

South		N	E	S	W
♠ J108		–	–	1H	1S
♥ AQ83		2D	NB	?	
♦ KJ					
♣ KQJ9					

You would like to play in 3NT but, obviously, your spades are not nearly good enough for you to suggest no-trumps now. By bidding 2S – the opponent's suit – you are asking partner to bid NTs if he holds something decent in that suit. This bid is 100% forcing, so if partner cannot help in spades, he must make another descriptive bid.

Bidding the opponent's suit is also used in response to take-out doubles and Overcalls (see Tip 42), where it is called an Unassuming Cue-bid.

A few years back. I was invited to a 12-man evening of serious social bridge. I knew no one but, early on, found myself in partnership with *The Tatler*'s witty bridge correspondent, John Graham, and I proceeded to take this advice to the extreme:

West (PM)	East (John Graham)	N	E	S	W
♠ KJ74	♠ AQ963	–	–	–	NB
♥ A986	♥ K732	3C	4C	5C	6C
♦ Q965	♦ AK104	NB	6S	all pass	
♣ 4	♣ –				

John and I had hurriedly agreed to play double for take-out over a pre-empt, so he had to be extra strong to bid 4C. Having passed, I felt that I could not have a more suitable hand, but, unable to decide what suit to play in, I thought I would ask John to pick whatever suit he preferred at the level I felt appropriate – namely, the 6-level. 6S was an excellent contract, and all four players had enjoyed bidding the same suit consecutively – not a regular occurrence at the bridge table.

7 / ALWAYS SUPPORT NO-TRUMPS WITH A LONG MINOR SUIT

In terms of the number of extra points you will score at the table, this tip has to be one of the most important in the book. The thought behind it lies firmly in the logic of avoiding playing in a minor suit Game contract at all costs. Take this typical hand for example:

West	East
♠ AJ8	♠ K5
♥ Q982	♥ J43
♦ Q43	♦ AK8752
♣ A32	♣ 86

West opens a Weak 1NT, and East should now consider the chances of Game. The simple choice appears to lie between 3NT and 5D. There are too few points even to contemplate 11 tricks. Nine tricks in 3NT, however, are well within the realms of possibility.

If you are addicted to points, then you should remember that **you can add on an extra point for every card over four in your long suit** when you are supporting NTs. This gives you a count of 13, and makes an immediate raise to 3NT seem obvious. If you think about it, providing that you are committed to making a Game contract, there really is no other bid.

In the final of the National Schools Championships – a long time ago – my partner, Quentin Moore, and I realised that we needed action to get back into the match. Opposite my 1NT opening, sitting East, he took this principle to the extreme, and came up with a raise to 3NT. I was not unhappy with his hand …

West	East
♠ A83	♠ –
♥ J1086	♥ 732
♦ AJ42	♦ 985
♣ K8	♣ AQJ7643

This turned out to be a massive swing because, not only did I make 3NT but, with clubs breaking 3-1, the opponents could make 4S – and our other pair had bid and made it! Not only did this redeem vital match points, but it stunned the opposition into an intense melancholia for the rest of the match.

Occasionally, when applying this rule, your 3NT will go three down. Ignore your partner's whining because, over time, this tip will make you a big winner.

8 / DON'T OPEN 4-4-4-1 HANDS WITH 12 OR 13 POINTS

World and European Championship reports are littered with words like 'catastrophe' and 'disaster'. Wherever these words appear it is almost certain that a dreaded 4-4-4-1 hand will not be far away.

In most natural bidding systems, opener's first two bids contain, by far, the largest amount of information that is imparted in any auction. This is particularly the case in Acol.

The problem with 4-4-4-1 hands is that, as they contain three features, they really need three bids to convey their content. In systems, like Acol, when you can't freely bid two different four-card suits, a considerable degree of lying is then involved. (Don't worry about this on moral grounds; lying at bridge is sometimes a very healthy option.)

The result of all this is that you frequently end in 4-3 trump fits (having to trump in your own hand) and hopeless misfit NT contracts, short on points.

The solution is a simple one: don't get yourself into this situation – **don't open the bidding with this distribution with only 12 or a poor 13pts.**

♠ 6
♥ AJ54
♦ KQJ3
♣ J632

Let's say you open 1H, and your partner responds 1S: you are now – to use a technical bridge term – stuffed. Whatever you bid now will be wrong – and wrong by some distance.

Don't open with this hand. Just pass. If partner bids, you will be back in action. If he bids 1S on a minimum opener, you will now stay out of a dodgy Game you would not have avoided had you opened. If he bids anything else, you can get excited.

If an opponent opens 1S, you have a perfect second round take-out double, which will delight your partner. If the opponents bid anything else, you were definitely right to pass.

In the long run, you will find yourself staying out of horrible contracts you wished you hadn't been faced with. With a classy 13pts (containing lots of tens and nines) or more, if your partner responds your singleton, you can re-bid NTs without risking so much – it is not perfect, but it's better …

The down-side to all this good news? A few missed part-scores … Missing Game is almost impossible: if partner cannot bid, what contract could you possibly have?

9 / WHEN VERY WEAK, BID IMMEDIATELY OPPOSITE A WEAK NT

One of the reasons the Strong NT has remained popular long past its sell-by date is because of disaster scares bandied about by players who have gone for big penalties opposite a doubled Weak NT. Of course, you can go for a number in an unfavourable situation, but then you can go for 1100 in a perfectly sensible contract too.

As usual, the headline-grabbing big penalties have swayed public opinion, whilst those dozens of hands where the Weak NT has pre-empted the opponents, occluded their 4-4 fit, or stolen the contract, are missed in the day-to-day hubbub of traffic across the green baize. The irony is that it is the very people who moan loudest about the dangers of the Weak NT who have caused the disasters.

♠ 6532
♥ 42
♦ J1098
♣ 432

If disaster awaits, don't sit there and accept it: spring into action. Here, your partner opens 1NT (12–14), and you hold this little beauty. Don't pass. If you do, you are inviting the next opponent to double for penalties. Instead, knowing that your opponents are due either a Game contract their way, or a big penalty, muddy their waters. Bid 2D now, as if you had five of them.

The advantage of an immediate bid is that a subsequent double by your opponents is now for take-out and, once they have bid, your side is out of trouble. You may still get caught in 2D doubled but, since neither opponent knows what is going on, it's unlikely.

If you play transfers, fire away as usual, without waiting for a five-card suit. If you want to bid 2C or 2D naturally, then you will have to wait for the second round, and take your chance.

Whenever you hold 0–3pts opposite a Weak NT, you should consider bidding something straight away if at all possible.

When the above hand cropped up at the table, playing on a simple systems night, my good friend Suzanne Saillard held the cards. She bid 2D, smoothly and confidently, the next opponent bid 2S, and was raised to 3S. There they played, making 11 tricks.

'What happened?' they said to one another.

Suzanne and I said not a word …

10 / OPEN THE WEAKER OF TWO FOUR-CARD MINOR SUITS

This tip is based on the premise that **when you open the bidding with a minor suit, it is almost always with your eye firmly on an eventual no-trump contract.**

West	East
♠ AJ8	♠ K105
♥ 102	♥ AK43
♦ AKQJ	♦ 8543
♣ 6532	♣ 104

My partner, Peter Hardyment, opened the West cards with 1C. I responded 1H. Peter re-bid 1NT (15–16), and I raised to 3NT without further ado.

After a short period of agonising, North decided to lead a low spade rather than fourth highest from ♣AJ983, and 10 tricks later, we were recording a top result on this hand.

This may all seem a little peculiar to the more honourable amongst you, but the principle is a sound one. When you are more likely to be misleading the opponents than your partner, it is no bad idea to tell the occasional lie. The success or failure of a no-trump contract is often down to the opening lead, so any advantage you can gain, you should.

This type of deception works well when used as an opening bid in a minor suit, because the likely final contract is a part-score in a minor – in which case trump quality is not all that important – or a NT Game. However, if you believe that you are heading for a Slam contract, it is usually right to bid where your values lie – this helps your partner judge the fit correctly. Not that the wily Zia Mahmood would necessarily agree. One of his notable swindles is the 'Sting Cue-bid', where he cue-bids a suit where he doesn't have the Ace, deliberately to mislead his opponents. I can't recommend such action to you; it usually leads to trouble – and not the sort of trouble you'll enjoy!

11 / WHEN TO JUMP-SHIFT

One of the soundest maxims for bidding is that when you know where you're going, go there fast, but, when you're not sure, take your time – using it to discover as much information as possible about the hand.

In the old days, it was mandatory to jump-shift in response to partner's opening bid with 16pts or more. Not so nowadays. Assume you hold the following hand, and your partner opens 1D:

♠ AQ854
♥ AK82
♦ 3
♣ A92

You hold a great hand but you have no idea in what denomination you will play or at what level. For this reason, bid slowly. Respond 1S, await partner's re-bid, and then, with the extra information, you will be well placed to judge how to proceed. You could use Fourth Suit Forcing, or bid a new suit at the 3-level.

When should you jump-shift? Only when you believe that there is a possible Slam contract, *and* you know in which suit it will be played. You will need either superb support for partner's suit, or a self-supporting suit of your own. You will need points, but 16+ is only an arbitrary figure. If you are a fan of the Losing Trick Count, look for hands with five losers or less.

Each of the following hands would be suitable for a jump-shift to 2S in response to an opening bid of 1H:

a	*b*	*c*
♠ AK872	♠ AKQJ987	♠ AKQ632
♥ AJ93	♥ Q3	♥ K9854
♦ 8	♦ A93	♦ –
♣ KJ6	♣ 2	♣ 96

In (a), you have wonderful support for partner. Whatever he re-bids, you then support hearts to set the trump suit in a Slam-going situation. **You also promise at least one of the top two honours in spades – the suit in which you jump-shifted.**

In (b), your spades are self-supporting. Whatever partner re-bids, you will bid spades again, categorically setting that suit as trumps, even if partner is void.

In (c), you have only 12pts, but amazing support and great distribution. Your partner needs to hold only A♣ and A♥ to make 7H a pretty solid Slam.

After each of these sequences, you can cue-bid, or approach your Slam by your pet methods. The jump-shift saves you bidding space in the long run, because it sets the suit, guarantees Game and implies a likely Slam.

When you do not have a fit with your partner, to jump would use up vital bidding space which could be used to discover the best final spot for your side.

12 / LOOK AT THE TEXTURE OF YOUR HAND TO HELP YOU JUDGE THE CONTRACT

Keep in mind that aces, kings, singletons and voids are great for suit contracts, but top cards are over-valued in no-trumps, whereas as Queens, Jacks, tens and nines are wonderful for no-trump contracts but, unless they are in the trump suit, much less useful in suit contracts.

You open 1NT and your partner bids 3S (natural and forcing). What do you re-bid?

♠ Q86
♥ QJ98
♦ K104
♣ AJ10

In Acol, you should bid 4S with three-card spade support or better, or 3NT if you hold a doubleton. Here, however, you need to think a little deeper. Your hand is completely flat and contains great values for a no-trump contract: Queens, Jacks, tens and nines. 3NT is definitely the recommended re-bid.

If your partner opened 1NT (12–14pts) and you held this hand, don't bother with Stayman – even if you have a 4-4 heart fit, 3NT is likely to be better.

Conversely, if you open 1S with this pile of rubbish, you should still have no hesitation in raising your partner's 3S limit raise to 4S. Your values are all suit-based: Aces, Kings and singletons.

♠ K86432
♥ 7
♦ A83
♣ A52

So, when faced with close decisions, look to the make-up of your hand to decide whether to play in a suit contract or in no-trumps.

For no-trumps, look for: Queens, Jacks, tens, nines, long minor suits. For suit contracts, look for: Aces, Kings, singletons and voids.

13 / HOW MANY POINTS MUST YOU HAVE TO USE STAYMAN?

Simple question. Simple answer: none. Next tip?

Perhaps not. Because for many people this answer will have come as something of a shock. They have been taught, and possibly played for years that, opposite a Weak NT, you need 11pts to use Stayman (7 or 8pts opposite a Strong NT).

On many occasions, this is right, because **when your partner gives you a response which does not please you, you must re-bid whatever you would have bid had you not used Stayman in the first place**. With balanced hands, this means at least 2NT. To make this bid, you need 11pts opposite a weak NT opening, or 7/8pts opposite a Strong NT.

However, there are many times when you have an *unbalanced* hand, and then you may be able to use Stayman to get out of a disgusting 1NT contract into something a little less unpalatable. With unbalanced hands, the only require-ment is that you can cope with *any* response your partner might give to the Stayman enquiry.

a	b	c
♠ 98642	♠ 6432	♠ J754
♥ Q982	♥ 7543	♥ KJ73
♦ 543	♦ J10986	♦ 9
♣ 2	♣ –	♣ J984

Each of these bids applies equally in response to a Strong or Weak NT, although their point is emphasised most greatly in response to the latter, because the trouble you are in is greater!

In (a), you could make a Weak Take-out into 2S. However, partner may hold two little spades, and four reasonable hearts. Using Stayman is quite safe. If partner responds 2D, you retreat into 2S – what you would have bid anyway – and this is still a Weak Take-out. If he responds 2H or 2S, you can pass, having found your best rescue suit.

In (b), Stayman is a much better alternative to bidding 2D immediately. Here, whatever your partner responds – including the 2D denial – you can pass, certain that you have found your best fit.

By the way, if you do pass 2D, your partner may suddenly seem a little nauseous, thinking you have forgotten the convention, but his face will regain some colour once he sees dummy and the clever bid you have made.

In (c), Stayman would be completely wrong, because although it would be fine and dandy if your partner responded 2H or 2S, you are completely stuck if he responds 2D. You must pass 1NT, and leave your partner to battle it out.

14 / YOU MUST HAVE EXACTLY FOUR CARDS IN A MAJOR SUIT TO USE STAYMAN

Stayman is one of the very few conventions I believe everyone should play. It is vital for the Rubber bridge player as it was designed specifically to locate a 4-4 fit in a major suit – the most desirable Game contract of all.

However, it is worth remembering that Stayman does not only *ask* partner whether he has a four-card major suit contained in his 1NT opener, it also *states* that you hold at least one four-card major in your own hand.

♠ KJ864
♥ AK4
♦ 93
♣ K32

Don't use Stayman on a hand like this. Bid a Game-forcing 3S (or a Transfer) to show a five-card suit. If partner holds three-card spade support, 4S will be the right spot; he does not need four-card support. Stayman should only be used when you have at least one four-card major suit in your hand. That means *exactly* four. For example, you might hold this:

♠ –
♥ KQJ3
♦ QJ98765
♣ A2

Here, you would employ Stayman opposite 1NT (12–14) to attempt to find a 4-4 heart fit. If that failed, you might decide to opt for 3NT or, more probably on this occasion, 5D. The key to this example is that it does not matter what else you have in your hand, there is just no point in using Stayman without a four-card major.

♠ KJ87
♥ KQ93
♦ 65
♣ A82

Because you are promising a four-card major when you use Stayman, the 1NT opener must be alert during a Stayman sequence too.

You open 1NT, partner bids 2C, and you respond 2H. Partner now jumps to 3NT. Don't be tempted to pass! Partner has promised a four-card major suit to use Stayman and, as it was not hearts, it must be spades. So, you should bid 4S. If your partner has used Stayman without a four-card major, you won't be pleased!

15 / DON'T LET THE OPPONENTS PLAY AT THE 1-LEVEL

Never let your opponents play at the 1-level. Well, I say 'never', but I mean almost never. If my opponents have a 60 part-score, and the bidding runs 1H-NB-NB around to me, I might leave them to make their 30pt score. If, at Duplicate Pairs, an opponent opens 1D and there are two passes to me and I hold 8pts with a singleton spade, I may suspect that they have missed a superior major suit contract and leave them to moulder in a minor-suit contract. However, these situations are relatively rare and, generally, if a 1-opener is being passed by responder, it is time to apply some pressure. Either your side has a making contract, or you need to push the opponents to an unsafe level.

	♠ 65432		**N**	**E**	**S**	**W**
	♥ 3		–	–	1H	NB
	♦ QJ98		NB	1S	2H	Dbl
	♣ 974		all pass			

♠ 9		♠ AJ1087
♥ K10864		♥ 9
♦ AK76		♦ 102
♣ KJ5		♣ 108632

	♠ KQ
	♥ AQJ752
	♦ 543
	♣ AQ

The key is that good competitive bidding is based on shape and not on points. If your partner is a good enough player to pass over an opponent's opening bid with a flat 14pts, then you must be good enough to 'protect' or 'balance' in the fourth seat, to ensure that you either steal the contract, or bully your opponents upwards.

This deal, from the semi-final of a big teams event, proved the point admirably. At Game All, South opened 1H, West correctly passed, and after two passes, East protected with a weak overcall of 1S. Now, when South re-bid 2H, West doubled for penalties. East gritted his teeth and passed. Best defence takes 800, but even the +500pts East-West achieved represented a substantial swing against the other table where East left 1H to play and fail by only one trick.

16 / DON'T LET THE OPPONENTS PLAY AT THE 2-LEVEL IF THEY HAVE FOUND A FIT

This rule will make a big difference to your scores – and to the respect which your opponents will show you in the future. Look at this auction:

N	E	S	W
1H	NB	2H	NB
NB	?		

South agrees hearts weakly; North can't even make a try for Game. However, they have found a fit and, if one side holds an eight-card fit, the other side virtually always has an eight-card fit too. The points will be close to 20–20 between E/W and N/S. When this occurs, never leave your opponents to play quietly at the 2-level. Bully them!

This hand demonstrates the principle:

North-South have found a fit and stopped in 2S. Should West bid now? Definitely, yes. Double is a possibility, but with a six-card suit, 3C is probably best. There are three main scenarios: N/S may defend and get you down (they won't double; they have a spade fit and limited points); they may bid on to 3S – if they make it, you have lost nothing; if they go down, you've pushed them out of a making part-score, and you may make 3C. None of these options looks bad. Only leaving them to play in 2S is the losing option.

Here, N/S can make 2S but not 3S, whilst E/W should secure nine tricks in 3C. You might argue that West was lucky to find partner with three good clubs but, on the other hand, N/S could scarcely have been stronger than 24pts to have passed out 2S.

17 / WHEN IS A DOUBLE FOR TAKE-OUT AND WHEN IS IT FOR PENALTIES?

This question provides vast opportunity for angst – even amongst top bridge players. Thankfully, for the Rubber bridge player, the distinction is not as clouded as you may fear.

Assuming that you are not playing a negative-style (Sputnik) double:

- if you have made a positive bid of any kind, then your partner's double is for penalties;
- if the opponent has opened 1NT, partner's double is for penalties;
- if the opponents have meandered up to a high level, partner's double is for penalties.

All other doubles are for take-out.

As you can see, there is no mention of rounds of bidding, or of whether partner has previously passed. These factors are irrelevant.

```
                 ♠ Q3                    N     E     S     W
                 ♥ KJ63                  –     –     1H    NB
                 ♦ 983                    3H    NB    NB    Dbl
                 ♣ KQJ4                   4H    Dbl
    ♠ AKJ9              ♠ 10765
    ♥ –                ♥ A10984
    ♦ J10765           ♦ 2
    ♣ 10987            ♣ 532
                 ♠ 842
                 ♥ Q752
                 ♦ AKQ4
                 ♣ A6
```

This hand demonstrates two different doubles within a short space of time:

Playing in a Swiss Teams final, South opened 1H and was raised to 3H by North. When South then passed, I, sitting West, came in to the action with a somewhat aggressive take-out double. North, seduced by his maximum, raised to 4H, and my partner, Norman Fried, doubled. Here, we had no difficulty with the doubles whatsoever: my double was take-out because my partner had not yet made a positive bid; Norman's double was penalties because I had made a positive bid.

There was even more conclusive evidence of their respective meanings to be gleaned from our trump holdings. With five hearts, Norman knew that I was void in hearts, and that my double must therefore be for take-out, whereas I, void in hearts, knew Norman had to be stacked.

So, **if you are in any doubt about the meaning of partner's double, your trump length may offer a vital clue**.

18 / A DOUBLE OF 1NT SHOULD ALWAYS BE FOR PENALTIES

This is another tip which will result in the occasional poor score, but will make you both rich and happy in the long run. My keenness for it was rewarded almost as soon as I had persuaded my partners to play it with me.

Playing Duplicate Pairs – all vulnerable – my RHO opened the bidding with a Weak NT, and I held this hand:

♠ AKQJ8
♥ AK4
♦ 43
♣ A32

I doubled, and there then followed three passes, the second of which, from my partner, I seem to remember was accompanied by a rather nervous swallow. Unadventurously, I bashed out my A♠, and was delighted to find dummy with a fairly balanced hand and 7pts. My miserable partner, marked now with a Yarborough, cheered up somewhat when I then cashed the first eight tricks, and claimed a 500pt penalty. The traveller, containing the results of the hand when it was played at previous tables, made for interesting reading. Every other pair sitting our way had lost points on the deal, playing in 3S-1, or 4S-2, sometimes doubled.

The reason for this is that players had either jumped to 3S (horrible, horrible) or had doubled 1NT. After the latter action, all the other players sitting with my partner's Yarborough had taken the bidding out into 2D, over which some number of spades were then bid.

Taking partner out of a penalty double over 1NT is a bad bet for two reasons. Firstly, the weaker you are, the more likely it is that partner's double is very strong – there is no upper limit for his bid.

Secondly, partner is saying that he thinks he can make seven tricks in defence to 1NT. By bidding, in effect, you are making the ridiculous statement that you think you are too weak to try to make seven tricks, so you will bid at the 2-level, where you need to make eight tricks … (I know this is simplifying the argument somewhat, but you see the point).

The statistic that should really convince you that this is a good policy is that, if the opponents make 1NT doubled (and they certainly will from time to time when you play this aggressively), you are only losing another 90pts (40 below, and 50 for the insult), whereas when you defeat them, you may be swinging over 1000pts your way.

So, keep your doubles of 1NT as showing a good 16pts or more – or seven certain tricks when on lead – and play it as a mandatory penalty double. If the partner of the 1NT opener redoubles, check carefully the meaning of this bid, before deciding whether to rescue partner, or continue penalising the opponents.

19 / OVER OPPONENT'S VULNERABLE 1NT, COMPETE IF YOU THINK YOUR SIDE HOLDS THE MINORITY OF THE POINTS; PASS AND DEFEND IF YOU THINK YOU HOLD THE MAJORITY

This advice is particularly valuable to Duplicate players, for whom every last point is vital. It should, however, help the Rubber and Chicago players to score a few more points too.

You would think that the ideal time to compete is when you are not vulnerable and the opponents are: even the description of this state of vulnerability – favourable – seems to suggest it. However, 1NT contracts, be they Strong or Weak openers, often fail and, if the opponents are vulnerable, scoring 100 or possibly 200 may be the best possible score for your side on the deal.

Put another way, if your side is making eight tricks you will score +200 if you defend 1NT (defeating it by two), and only +90 or +110 if you play at the 2-level in your minor or major suit, respectively. Defending looks a good deal now. However, it is not nearly so good when the opponents are not vulnerable as you are dividing those penalties in half.

So, if you think your side has the majority of the points, you should often pass.

South	N	E	S	W
♠ 83	–	1NT	?	
♥ AQJ85				
♦ A32				
♣ K76				

This is a dangerous situation at which to risk an overcall of 2H. You may get doubled for a sizeable penalty and, if East is vulnerable, you have very little to gain by bidding. If your side can make Game, you will be defeating 1NT by masses: if West makes a weak take-out, you can come in with 2H later, when it is much safer. Most importantly, as your side may hold the majority of the points on this deal, you should relish the opportunity to defend a vulnerable 1NT with this hand. You are on lead with your long suit, and with the outside entries in order to enjoy it.

South	N	E	S	W
♠ QJ9876	–	–	–	1NT
♥ 4	NB	NB	?	
♦ A832				
♣ 6				

Here's the flipside:

With two passes to you after the 1NT opening, it seems likely that your side holds the minority of the points on this deal. (If North had been very weak he should have bid – see Tip 9.) You should bid 2S, which, non-vulnerable and with a six-card suit, is quite safe. Even if your partner raises you, you should not be dismayed: partner knows you could be weak, having read Tip 15.

By adopting these methods, you will steal the contract when it is right to do so, and when your opponents are going down, show no mercy in defence of their contract.

20 / NEVER USE BLACKWOOD WITH A VOID

There is a certain type of player who always wants to be in control. He most wants to play the hand but, if he can't, he wants to show that it was *he* who bid the Slam, or *he* who found the killing lead … He is a tiresome character indeed for, although there is scope for individual prowess, bridge remains one of the greatest partnership games ever invented.

Playing in a recent Rubber bridge game, the following hand was held by my LHO. Her partner opened 1H, and I passed. She took control immediately: she was a much better player than her partner – she had told us all that after the very first hand. But what should she respond?

West
♠ AKQ76
♥ AJ985
♦ KQJ
♣ –

It is, truly, a mighty good hand to hold opposite an opening bid. A small Slam seems certain, and 13 tricks very possible, but, before speaking, assess what cards you really need for the grand Slam.

Clearly 7H seems most likely to be the best 13-trick spot. So, the King of trumps is vital and, if partner holds only four hearts, the Queen of trumps too. (Five-card major players can relax on this one, at least.) Other than these, A♦ is the last vital card. A♣ would be waste-paper – there are no club losers in the hand, and not even a useful discard to be taken.

The villain of this piece launched directly into Blackwood. Her partner responded 5D – showing one Ace – but was it the crucial A♦ or the redundant A♣? She bid 6H forlornly and, seconds later, her partner spread the hand – 7H was laydown.

And therein lies the key reason why you should not use Blackwood with a void. It should be used only when you are interested in *how many* Aces partner holds. Cue-bidding should be applied when you wish to know *which* Aces partner holds. Having discovered that partner held A♦, she could then use Roman Key-Card Blackwood (see Tip 21) to assess the trump position. Bidding the Grand Slam would be easy.

The correct auction might run something like this:

N	E	S	W	
–	1H	NB	2S	* natural suit re-bid
NB	3C*	NB	3H	> cue-bid denying A♣, but
NB	4D>	NB	4NT	showing A♦
NB	5S^	NB	7H	^ RKCB, showing A♦, ♥KQ

21 / UPGRADE TO ROMAN KEY-CARD BLACKWOOD

This version of Blackwood is so good, I have taken to teaching it directly to my beginners; when they see old-fashioned Blackwood, they scoff at how primitive it is. The beauty of RKCB is that, as well as Aces, it informs you about the King and Queen of trumps – both vital cards at the Slam level. There are several variations and complex additions, but the simple method outlined below is perfect for Rubber bridge and club Duplicate players. I urge you to replace old-fashioned Blackwood immediately.

Instead of Aces, the 4NT bid asks for 'key-cards'. These are the four Aces, plus the trump King. The responses to the 4NT enquiry are as follows:

5C = I hold 0 or 3 key-cards
5D = I hold 1 or 4 key-cards
5H = I hold 2 key-cards, but not the trump Queen
5S = I hold 2 key-cards, and also the trump Queen

You will not confuse no key-cards with three key-cards (nor one with four) – there is at least 11pts between them. In all the years I have played this convention, I have always known which my partner holds – and that is saying something: I have got everything else wrong at some point!

Both 5H and 5S show two key-cards – the most common number of key-cards held. The lower-ranking bid denies the trump Queen; the higher-ranking bid shows this card.

Once you know that you hold all five key-cards – and only if you are interested in bidding a grand Slam – a bid of 5NT asks partner for Kings but, crucially, not how many, but which one(s). When bidding a grand Slam, you usually need an exact King.

In response to 5NT, you bid the suit in which you hold a King, not including the trump King which has already been shown in response to 4NT: if you hold two Kings, bid 6NT; if you hold no King, go back to the agreed suit at the lowest available level.

West	N	E	S	W
♠ K5	–	–	–	1H
♥ K8643	NB	3H	NB	4NT
♦ AKQ72	NB	5S	NB	7H
♣ A				

When partner raises you to 3H, to use RKCB seems sensible. His response of 5S shows two key-cards, plus the trump Queen. The key cards must be A♥ and A♦. You do not need to worry about the fourth and fifth diamonds: you are bound to be able to establish the suit. As Grand Slams go, knowing that partner holds the trump Queen makes this one pretty easy to bid.

22 / KEEP YOUR PRE-EMPTS PURE FIRST AND SECOND IN HAND

You pick up your best hand of the day, and partners open with a pre-empt? It happens so often and it leaves you with a prickly problem.

Experts recognise the value of keeping pre-empts up to standard *before* their partner has bid, in case it is he who holds the strong hand.

The successful pre-empt hand has high suit quality, but almost no values outside. As you are gambling being doubled for a sizeable penalty against the opponents finding and making the right Game contract, it makes sense to have little defence to their contract. If you hold good cards in defence, why gamble with a pre-empt?

If you want to pre-empt before your partner has had a chance to speak, your hand should conform to a pre-arranged minimum standard: a seven-card suit, headed by three of the five honours, including Ace *or* King: no more than one outside Queen, or a couple of Jacks.

Now your partner can judge accurately when to go for Game, when to support and continue the pre-empt, when to pass, when to double the opponents. He can respond 3NT with as little as Ax or Kx in your suit because he knows that your suit is of sufficient quality to make it produce seven tricks most of the time. (This is why you should not hold both Ace **and** King in the suit. Firstly, you are quite defensive with this holding and, secondly, your partner will find it difficult to bid 3NT without either top honour.)

Third (or fourth) in hand, your pre-empts can be as reckless as your style dictates. A passed partner can say nothing other than raise you pre-emptively.

a	b	c
♠ KQJ10987	♠ K62	♠ 42
♥ 4	♥ Q986432	♥ 7
♦ 432	♦ Q3	♦ AK97542
♣ 83	♣ 4	♣ Q104

You deal, and pick up these hands: On which would you pre-empt with a Weak-3 Opener in first or second position?

Hand (a) is a perfect first or second hand 3S pre-empt – high-quality suit, nothing outside.

Hand (b) is hideous. Dire suit quality, defensive tricks in the outside suits. You are taking a great risk for little gain – and you may be doubled and lose thousands of points!

Hand c is unsuitable because you hold ♦AK, making it tough for partner to bid 3NT. Also, the pre-empt is unlikely to stop the opponents reaching 4H or 4S and, by opening 3D, you might tip them off to the bad distribution. Pass or open 1D.

Of course, by disciplining yourself to pre-empting with only certain hands, you reduce the frequency with which you can open a Weak-3.

I propose that the increase in accuracy will more than compensate the lack of action.

23 / THREE MINI-TIPS ON PRE-EMPTS

1 Don't open a pre-empt with an outside Ace

The requirement to hold an outside Ace in order to make a pre-empt is decades out of date. In modern Acol – and other systems too – bidding has become more aggressive and competitive. With outside values, you are simply too strong to make a pre-empt, a bid which should be reserved for hands with a high-quality seven-card suit, and less than 10pts.

2 A pre-emptive overcall must be made at the third available level

East	N	E	S	W
♠ 982	1S	4C		
♥ 8				
♦ 5				
♣ KQJ108654				

The key to identifying a pre-empt in any position is by the level at which the bid is made in relation to any other bids. A bid at the 3-level is not automatically a pre-empt – but a bid at the third *available* level is.

So, if your RHO opens 1S, and you have eight clubs, and wish to pre-empt, you cannot just bid 3C and expect partner to understand (that would be a jump-overcall). You must overcall 4C, because that is the third available level for your suit. Naturally, when vulnerable, you must ensure that the risk is worth the gain, and keep your suit quality very high.

3 Don't pre-empt in a new suit if your partner has opened the bidding

East	N	E	S	W
♠ 982	–	1C	NB	1H
♥ AQJ8743				
♦ J5				
♣ 4				

As the purpose of a pre-empt is to use up the opponents' bidding space, it really is illogical to make a pre-empt in response to your partner's opening bid. It wastes your own space, and usually results in the wrong contract.

The one time when you would pre-empt opposite your partner's opening bid is when you hold a weak hand with big support for his suit (see Tip 2).

24 / HAVING PRE-EMPTED, NEVER BID AGAIN

If you analyse most bidding disasters at social bridge you find that they are attributable to overbidding. Not just getting too high, but bidding your hand too many times. **Once you've described what you have in your hand, you must pass.** Shock though it may be to some, you have a partner, and you must trust him to have heard what you've said, and to judge whether to continue in the auction.

This sequence is typical of what happens all too often:

N	E	S	W
3C	3S	NB	4S
5C!	Dbl	All Pass	

What on earth is North doing? He has described a weak hand with a seven-card suit, and it must now be up to his partner to decide whether or not to sacrifice against 4S.

If North is really prepared to compete at the 5-level, he should have opened 5C in the first place, because bidding it slowly has allowed his opponents time to exchange information and then decide, in comfort, whether to bid on or double him. Besides, North has no idea what is going on. Perhaps E/W are not making 4S, or maybe they are making 6S. South is in a far better position to judge this, so leave it to him.

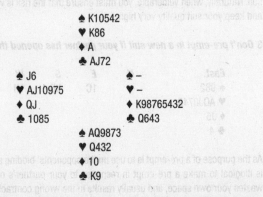

This extraordinary hand occurred in the first match of the inaugural Macallan Club Teams Championship.

Top expert, Glyn Liggins, East, opened 5D, and N/S, Elizabeth & Tony Fathers, did well to stop in 5S. Liggins was not remotely tempted to bid on with his remarkable 9-4 distribution, correctly leaving it to his partner, Willie Whittaker, to make the decision.

5S making might seem a poor result, but in the other room East opened with a crafty 3D and, with a little encouragement from partner, bid on and on to 7D over 6S by N/S. Andrew Robson and Peter Hardyment, sitting N/S, had no difficulty in doubling and defeating this by four tricks to gain a valuable swing for their teams' discipline.

25 / RESPONDING TO A PRE-EMPT – THE KEY ELEMENTS

Your partner opens 3H. What should you respond with this hand?

♠ AK4
♥ K
♦ A973
♣ J9832

Do not be tempted to respond 3NT since, with no outside entry, you may be unable to enjoy partner's long heart suit. Instead, opt to bid 4H. You have an eight-card trump fit and useful Aces and Kings, making the major-suit Game far safer and more likely to succeed.

What about your response to an opening 3C bid on this hand?

♠ A64
♥ A43
♦ A93
♣ A832

5C? Perhaps 6C? Neither is likely to make. However, there is one Game contract odds-on to succeed: 3NT. Partner has a high-quality seven-card suit, headed by either A♣ or K♣, so you have seven certain club tricks, plus three Aces. That's 10 tricks, and partner quite definitely isn't promising an 11th!

- After a major-suit pre-empt, support partner's suit, or pass. Don't go for NTs.
- After a minor-suit pre-empt, head for NTs, but you must hold at least Ax or Kx in the suit, preferably three to an honour. This way, you can be sure that your partner's suit can be developed, even in a hand with no outside entries.

Although it rarely happens:

- a change of suit is 100% forcing, and suggests a genuine alternative trump suit. Opener should support with a doubleton, or return to his own suit with a singleton or void.

26 / AFTER OPPONENT'S PRE-EMPT, DON'T STRETCH TO BID SLAM CONTRACTS

When an opponent tries to ruin your auction, it is a natural instinct to want to make him pay. However, it is worth reflecting that their aggression has tipped you off to a very important factor – peculiar distribution. For, if there is one seven-card suit openly reported, there are usually other horrors awaiting their chance to rear up and surprise you.

This hand from the inaugural playing of the Queen's Centenary Cup helped the expert team to victory against five club teams:

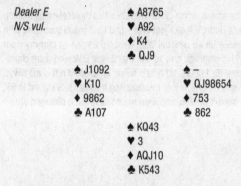

Dealer E
N/S vul.

```
                    ♠ A8765
                    ♥ A92
                    ♦ K4
                    ♣ QJ9
   ♠ J1092                        ♠ –
   ♥ K10                          ♥ QJ98654
   ♦ 9862                         ♦ 753
   ♣ A107                         ♣ 862
                    ♠ KQ43
                    ♥ 3
                    ♦ AQJ10
                    ♣ K543
```

Playing South against the team from Queen's Club, Jeremy Flint doubled East's extremely aggressive non-vulnerable 3H pre-empt for take-out, and West passed. Irving Rose, sitting North, not renowned for underbidding, considered his bid for some time (a similarly rare occurrence), before bidding a modest 4S.

At the other table East, Tony Priday, passed first in hand, and N/S meandered their way up to 6S, which failed on the unpleasant 4-0 trump break.

Of course, the bad split was unlucky, but Rose had obviously been warned off by East's pre-empt.

Dealer West	♠ AJ		
N/S Game	♥ AK10987		
	♦ 10		
	♣ KJ102		

	N	E	S	W
	–	–	–	3D
	3H	5D	5S	NB
	6S	NB	7S	NB
	NB	Dbl		

West hand:
♠ 106
♥ 6432
♦ KQJ8543
♣ —

East hand:
♠ 96
♥ —
♦ 9762
♣ Q987643

South hand:
♠ KQ85432
♥ QJ5
♦ A
♣ A3

This deal reinforces the advice. North-South overstretched themselves by bidding the Slam – although, *a priori*, it looks just fine – and East made them pay with a Lightner Double, asking for an unusual lead. West led 2♥; when dummy went down, South claimed his contract, only to find that it was E/W who were claiming – the first four tricks: East could ruff hearts twice; West could ruff clubs twice.

E/W rubbed South's nose in it further by observing that had N/S stayed in 6S, there wouldn't have been a double, and West would have led a diamond …

27 / RESPONDING TO AN OVERCALL

Good bridge players adopt different systems all over the world. However, when all good players agree to play the same methods, you know that they have discovered the best treatment for a particular situation. So it is when it comes to responding to an overcall.

Most of the time, partner overcalls to start a barrage of the opponents' auction. He wants you to support that barrage to use up bidding space and pressurise your opponents.

When responding to an overcall, the maxim 'support or shut-up' is correct 98% of the time. If you do not like your partner's suit, unless very strong, you should pass.

When you can support partner's suit (three-card support is ample) your responses are divided into two categories:

- If you believe your side has the majority of points between you, and you might be able to make Game, start with an Unassuming Cue-bid (see Tip 42).
- If you feel that your side has the minority of the points, follow this advice:

In a competitive auction, it is your trump length – and not points – which should decide how high you are prepared to compete: usual bidding requirements are lifted. Providing that you have either some points in trumps, or some decent distribution, just follow the Total Trump Principle: **bid as many tricks as you hold trumps between you.**

This does not mean you will make this number of tricks – you have the minority of the points – but it will get you into the highest **safe** contract available.

a	b	c
♠ K74	♠ K742	♠ KJ742
♥ 86	♥ 6	♥ 6
♦ Q9652	♦ Q9652	♦ 96542
♣ 984	♣ 984	♣ 94

In these examples, your LHO has opened 1H; your partner has overcalled 1S and RHO has then bid 2C (forcing):

In (a), you know that your side holds eight spades between you, and you should therefore bid to an eight-trick contract immediately, namely 2S.

In (b), you hold nine trumps between you, so you should bid 3S immediately.

In (c), you have 10 trumps, so you could bid 4S straight away.

It is important to jump directly, as this causes maximum disruption. Note that you hold no more points for your jump to 4S than you did for your simple raise to 2S. This is because when your side holds the minority of points, trump length is your only concern.

28 / NEVER BID AT THE 5-LEVEL WITHOUT 10 TRUMPS BETWEEN YOU

One great problem in competitive bidding is knowing when to stop. If I knew a rule that could help you make the right decision every time, I would have won far more rubbers than I have, but this tip should help you avoid most of the disasters and, funnily enough, that is what being a good player is all about.

It is the first hand of the rubber and, sitting East, you open 1H. The next chance you have to bid, your opponents are already up at 4S. What do you say?

East	N	E	S	W
♠ 82	–	1H	1S	3H
♥ KQ98	4S	?		
♦ KJ65				
♣ AQ6				

If it were me, I'd double. That's not a mandatory penalty, but just a bid to show a strong hand, only four hearts, and a determination not to let my opponents play in 4S undoubled. If my partner has brilliant distribution, he can bid on. Otherwise, we'll take the money in 4S doubled.

As described in the previous tip, the competitive auction is all about trump length. The ideal situation is to bid to as many tricks as you hold trumps between you but, in fact, it will work fine to bid one more trick than you have trumps. Therefore, if you want to bid an 11-trick contract, 5H, you've got to believe that you have at least 10 trumps. Here, that is most unlikely, so a double is marked.

Incidentally, one exception to this rule would be when you know you hold an eight-card fit – or bigger – in two suits. That double fit always produces extra tricks for you.

I gave this tip to two of my favourite students before they played in a big event. They went on to win it, but when questioned on their mistakes, they sheepishly confessed that the two really bad hands they'd played both featured them up at the 5-level without the requisite 10 trumps!

Finally, a tip from US International Michael Rosenberg: at Teams of Four, or Rubber bridge, never sacrifice. If you get it wrong (because your opponents couldn't make their contract) you have made a huge mistake.

29 / THE GAMBLING 3NT OPENER IS A GAMBLE IN YOUR FAVOUR

It helps to have a gambling instinct at the bridge table, providing it is matched by the discipline to stick to the rules and play the odds. Above all, never be afraid of losing. If you are fearless, you will win far more often.

The Acol Gambling 3NT Opening (there are similar versions in most bidding systems) is a tremendously powerful tool combining, as it does, a vicious pre-empt with the opportunity to score a slim Game contract.

To open with 3NT, you must hold a solid (headed by AKQJ) seven-card minor suit, and scattered values in the outside suits. Do not have too much outside your strong suit, as this makes the pre-emptive nature of the bid less effective and you move into Strong Two opening territory. Outside your suit, one King, or the odd Queen and Jack, is maximum.

In response, unless partner can see a superior Game or Slam contract, he should pass. If the opening is doubled, and responder cannot stand 3NT, he normally bids 4C. If this is your suit you pass; if not, you bid 4D. In this contract, you will have seven certain tricks (plus honours at Rubber bridge), and if your partner can provide no more, the opponents must have a Game or Slam available to them.

West	a) East	b) East	c) East
♠ 83	♠ A62	♠ 542	♠ K5
♥ 64	♥ A9832	♥ 753	♥ AKQ53
♦ Q4	♦ J1097	♦ AK542	♦ AK962
♣ AKQJ1083	♣ 4	♣ 75	♣ 2

The hand on the left (West) opens 3NT, and the next hand passes. What should you respond with each of the East hands?

a) Pass. Partner has seven club tricks and you hold two Aces. Your diamonds form a stopper and 3NT will make.

b) 4C. You must rescue your partner, who might lose the first 10 tricks in the major suits if left in 3NT. 4C will only fail by one trick at most which, considering your opponents may well have a 4H or 4S available to them, is a great result.

c) 6C. Yep, you read that right. You can count 12 tricks: seven in clubs, two in diamonds, three in hearts. The problem lies in which Slam to bid. 6NT is very risky because, if the opponents lead spades, your K♠ is exposed, and you may lose five or six tricks immediately. You want the lead coming around to your hand to protect your unguarded K♠. As you know your partner has solid clubs, bidding a Slam with a singleton trump is not quite as *avant garde* as it may first appear. Now, you will make 12 tricks even if the opponents do lead spades.

The former bridge club owner, Stefan Stefan, wittily boasted that there is a Polish Gambling 3NT Opener. In this version, you show two tricks and hope that your partner has the remaining seven! NB: He is making a joke.

30 / IF YOU DISCOVER A MISFIT – STOP BIDDING. DON'T BID NO-TRUMPS!

When I was learning this Game, Pat Cotter, my predecessor at *The Financial Times*, asked me to partner him one afternoon. As well as having the opportunity to play way above my level – the best way to learn – I was also given a simple piece of advice which has stood me in good stead ever since. I was sitting South, holding this collection. And the bidding ran as follows:

South		N	S
♠ 8		1S	2D
♥ K42		2S	?
♦ AQ6532			
♣ J76			

All my instincts told me to pass, but I didn't want to leave my partner in a rotten contract. So, I bid 3D. This did save Pat from a poor contract, but it put me in a worse one – and we were lucky not to be doubled. I went two down, and asked partner if I should have passed. He told me what I suppose I already knew: don't bid on with a misfit, just pass, and keep the level low.

The worst crime of all is to bid no-trumps, trying to rescue a misfit auction. Now, you have no source of tricks and no entries to get from one hand to the other.

A few months later I was playing against two nervous ladies. On the first of our two hands, the bidding ran like this:

South		N	S
♠ KJ432		1H	1S
♥ 2		2H	2S
♦ A32		**3H**	
♣ Q762			

Not surprisingly, 3H was not a good spot and, when South turned to enquire what she should have done, flushed with my little knowledge, I suggested that she should have passed 2H. My partner, who was a better player than me, looked none too pleased, so I subsided, and got on with the next hand. This was it:

South	N	S
♠ –	1S	2D
♥ 942	2S	**NB**
♦ AJ532		
♣ AJ762		

This time our opponents stopped in 2S and, although they went one down, it was still the best result for them. Most pairs were in 3S, or 4C, and one was even three off in 3NT doubled.

'Well,' said my opponent sweetly, 'your advice worked nicely that time ...'

So, not only were Pat Cotter's words vindicated yet again, but I had learnt another lesson, which I now pass on to you as a bonus tip:

Don't give advice to your opponents until after you have finished playing with them.

31 / IF YOU DON'T KNOW WHAT TO BID IN AN UNCONTESTED AUCTION, BID THE FOURTH SUIT

If you are bidding in a competitive auction, and you can't decide what to bid, you can always bid the opponents' suit to wake partner up (see Tip 6).

When the auction is uncontested, you still have two unconditionally forcing bids you can make to find out more about partner's hand: bidding a new suit at the 3-level is 100% forcing, unless you have responded 1NT initially (see Tip 3).

Best of all, you have Fourth Suit Forcing (4SF) – an essential part of any system. Bidding the fourth suit is not natural because, if you had held good cards there, you would have bid No-trumps (see Tip 5). Instead, it tells partner that you have a Game-going hand (or better) but you do not know what to bid, and you want him to describe his hand further.

South	N	S
♠ 85	1S	2D
♥ K42	2H	?
♦ AK652		
♣ K76		

Here, South cannot support either of partner's suits, nor re-bid his own – it would show a six-card suit. He must not bid No-trumps either, as this would promise two stoppers in the unbid suit. Instead, the correct bid is 3C – Fourth Suit Forcing – which tells partner that he has an opening hand, but does not know what to bid next. North now describes his hand further. If he holds extra cards in spades or hearts, he re-bids that suit. If he has a stopper in clubs, he can bid NTs. If he has three-card support for partner's diamonds, he can now support those.

If he has nothing else to say, he just returns to his first suit, and South is left to guess the best contract. Most of the time, however, South will gain a vital new piece of information with which he can judge the right final spot.

To use 4SF at the 1 or 2-level, you need 11/12pts or more, and you *suggest* that you hold one stopper in the fourth suit. If you use 4SF at the 3-level, this is Game-forcing, and *promises* a stopper in the suit. So, if partner also has one stopper, no-trumps will be safe.

This was a super 4SF sequence which resulted in a match-winning Slam:

West	East	W	E
♠ AJ85	♠ K6	1C	1D
♥ 2	♥ A753	1S	2H
♦ 952	♦ AKQ743	3D	4NT
♣ AK964	♣ 8	5H	**7D**

West's 1S re-bid showed 5-4 distribution so, when East used 4SF, West's 3D bid confirmed his shape as 5-4-3-1. The news that West held a singleton heart was music to East's ears, as he now knew that he could trump his little hearts with West's trumps. Playing standard Blackwood, West's 5H showed two Aces, and East bid the excellent 28pt Grand Slam confidently.

Not only will 4SF ease the bidding and keep you out of the bad contracts, its brilliant shape-showing qualities will ensure that you reach some slim distributional contracts too. If you don't already play it, its addition to your system should net you hundreds of points in a very short time.

32 / THE SIMPLE LOSING TRICK COUNT

The Losing Trick Count (LTC) is a method of evaluating your cards either as an alternative, or in addition, to a point-count system like Acol. Most experts use it as a double-check when deciding to what level they can safely bid.

In its simple form, the LTC should only be used once you know you have a fit, and you want to decide whether to bid at the 2, 3, or 4-level. It is used ideally with a 4-4 or 5-4 trump fit – as the fit becomes more unbalanced, or you have more trumps, the LTC becomes less accurate.

Let's see how it works: the LTC works by counting a loser for every one of the top three honours missing from each suit, up to the number of cards you hold there (i.e., if you only hold a doubleton, you cannot have more than two losers). You then make an assumption about your partner's likely number of losers, and bid accordingly.

As a responder, you should assume that an opening partner will hold seven losers or less (this covers most opening hands). You add your losers to this number, and subtract the total from 18. The resulting figure gives you the level to which you are safe to bid.

West	East
♠ AQ842	♠ K975
♥ 2	♥ 9853
♦ AK43	♦ Q87
♣ 932	♣ A4
6 losers	8 losers

West opens 1S, and East is borderline between a raise 2S or 3S. With two losers in spades, three in hearts, two in diamonds, and one in clubs. East can add his eight losers to West's expected seven losers, making 15. This, subtracted from 18, leaves three, suggesting that 3S is the correct bid.

West, with only six losers instead of the seven East was assuming, can therefore raise to 4S. Notice that West's six losers and East's eight losers total 14. Take this from 18, and the 4-level is now shown to be correct.

There are many adjustments and advances that can be made should you wish to adopt the LTC more regularly. Consult a book dedicated to the subject.

33 / ADD POINTS FOR SHORTAGES ONLY ONCE YOU HAVE FOUND A FIT

This tip may be too basic for many readers, but I have seen too many players add distribution points at the wrong time, so perhaps it is well to check for any bad habits.

When opening or overcalling, you may add extra points for a long suit(s). Generally, you add 1pt for each card over four in your long suit. No points should be counted for shortages as yet, because if partner holds length in that suit, your shortage is bad news, not good.

If you support partner's suit, or your suit is supported by partner, then shortages are definitely working, because you have sufficient trumps to use for ruffing. However, because you usually wish to trump in only one hand (the one which is shorter in trumps), leaving the other, longer, hand to draw trumps, the scale of additional points is different, when you are supporting partner, from when you have been supported.

	When supported	Having been supporting
void	+5	+3
singleton	+3	+2
doubleton	+1	+1

Notice the higher values for shortages when your hand is likely to be dummy – the place to make useful ruffs. The more modest values for shortages in the declarer hand indicate that ruffing in hand is usually something you only do when forced by the opponents.

a	b
♠ K872	♠ K8752
♥ 932	♥ –
♦ J75	♦ J7
♣ QJ6	♣ QJ6542

Contrast these two hands after partner has opened the bidding with 1S:

In (a), you are barely worth the raise to 2S. Your balanced hand contains no opportunity for ruffing whatsoever.

In (b), your hand is wonderfully suited to playing in spades. You can add an extra point for the fifth trump, and 5pts for the heart void. Added to your seven high card points, you now have the equivalent of 13pts, so you jump to 4S straight away – and expect partner to make it.

34 / OVERCALL 1NT WITH UNBALANCED HANDS TOO

A standard overcall of 1NT shows a balanced 16–18pts. However, there are some strategic advantages to overcalling 1NT with another type of hand also: one with a long, high-quality minor suit. Not only can this overcall help you to reach 3NT – which, with a long minor suit, should be in your mind – but also intimidate and discourage your opponents.

Take a look at this hand from the first round of the Gold Cup:

Dealer South	♠ A10953		
N/S Game	♥ J3		
	♦ A2		
	♣ 8642		

N	E	S	W
–	–	1H	1NT
NB	NB	NB	

♠ 87		♠ 642
♥ A5		♥ 8764
♦ 976		♦ Q1054
♣ AKQJ75		♣ 93

♠ KQ4
♥ KQ1092
♦ KJ83
♣ 10

Over South's opening 1H bid, my partner, Sajid Ispahani, opted to overcall 1NT – and this was passed out. North led J♥ and Saj took his A♥ and six clubs to claim his contract. This was a great result for us since North-South could have both defeated 1NT and, more importantly, made 4S.

North should definitely have doubled West's 1NT overcall to show a decent hand but, even then, West can bid 2C which fails by only one trick, and Game is far from easy for N/S to reach.

There is one further observation to be made about this hand: if the North and East hands are swapped, E/W would have bid 3NT – via showing his five-card spade suit – and that makes also.

When you have a solid minor suit, you may overcall 1NT with only a single stopper in the opponent's suit. Notice that, if you add two extra points for your fifth and sixth club, you have 16pts anyway, so this frisky style of overcall is far from outrageous. Of course, from time to time, your opponents may get the better of you, but, in the long run, this style of aggression pays off very well, especially for Duplicate Pairs players.

35 / MAKE VERY AGGRESSIVE OVERCALLS IF YOUR SUIT IS SPADES

An overcall is the start of a barrage; if partner can support you, he does. This barrage is at its most effective when the overcalled suit is spades; the highest ranking suit forcing the opponents to a higher level. For this reason, you should be keen to make a light overcall if your suit is spades.

♠ AJ10753
♥ 984
♦ 3
♣ 982

RHO opens 1C; you should overcall 1S. This cuts out all the 1-level suit responses for responder. 1S is particularly effective because it is over a 1C opener; over a 1H opening, you could still overcall 1S, but it is less destructive.

Many pairs who play Duplicate have adopted weak jump-overcalls as part of their system. On the hand above, they would bid 2S, immediately increasing the effect of the barrage. If your partner had already passed, and the vulnerability was favourable, you might even bid 3S!

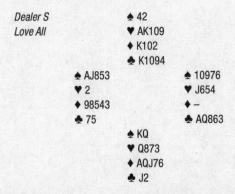

This next hand proved a vital board in the English Bridge Union's Swiss Pairs Championship:

Sitting N/S were England Internationals David Price and Peter Crouch. When South opened 1D my partner, Peter Hardyment, overcalled 1S and, over North's negative double, I raised to 3S. This left N/S – who held a combined 28 count – with the problem. South doubled, and 3S was left to play. Despite the good trump lead from North, partner still managed to scramble nine tricks for the best result – no other E/W pair played the hand in 3S doubled.

3NT is easy for N/S, and even 4H made some of the time.

36 / PRE-EMPT MORE AGGRESSIVELY THIRD IN HAND

Never let your opponents feel relaxed playing against you; that makes the game too easy. Keep them harried and uncomfortable, uncertain of vital information.

If your partner and right-hand opponent have already passed, and you hold a sub-minimum opening hand, the chances are that your LHO holds a sizeable opening hand. To prevent him from describing that hand accurately would provide you with a big advantage.

Personally, I'm not a fan of opening light third-in-hand at the 1-level (unless I hold a six-card suit). I find that this provides very little obstruction, and often results in partner misjudging what to do later. However, to pre-empt third-in-hand, with fewer cards, and with a wider range of point counts, is far more obstructive.

Assuming that the vulnerability is either Love All, or that your opponents are vulnerable and you are not, what would you bid after two passes to you?

a	b	c
♠ 87	♠ QJ9843	♠ 7
♥ 86	♥ 6	♥ QJ109876
♦ KQJ985	♦ 92	♦ 9654
♣ A74	♣ J985	♣ 2

a) To open with 1D creates no pressure on your opponents and may even help them to reach and make their major-suit contract. Open 3D to cause problems.
b) Holding only 4pts opposite a passed hand means that your opponents definitely have a Game contract available. Open 3S to make reaching 3NT very tough and 4H more difficult.
c) Again, Game is a certainty for your opponents; even a Slam is possible. Open 4H to prevent both 3NT and, hopefully, 4S contracts and make life very difficult for your opponents.

Notice that suit length is compromised by one on each occasion. Your partner should be aware that pre-empts third-in-hand may be a card short and he should be reluctant to bid anything in response, reasoning that your pre-empt has caused sufficient damage.

Be prepared to play in a few doubled contracts. Even if they fail dramatically from time to time, in the long run you will find that your aggression pays dividends, and builds your reputation as difficult to play against.

37 / SUPPORT PARTNER'S MAJOR SUIT ON THREE CARDS RATHER THAN RESPONDING 1NT

For players of five-card major systems, this advice should be obvious. For players whose partners can open 1H or 1S with only four cards, it is an important tip both technically and strategically.

The two elements which contribute to this thinking are these:

- a 1NT response should be reserved for very weak hands where a major suit contract is unsuitable, and where you do not want your partner re-bidding his major suit without six of them;
- a raise in a major suit is more pre-emptive than a response of 1NT. If partner is weak, the opponents are likely to come into the auction. If he is strong, he will not be disappointed to have been supported.

♠ K74
♥ 92
♦ QJ32
♣ 7632

Playing Acol, where you never open a four-card spade suit if you have another four-card suit available, if partner does open 1S, he will have five or more over 95% of the time; the remaining times, he will have 15pts or more and a 4-3-3-3 shape.

If he has five spades, 2S is definitely right; if he has the flat hand, a response of 2S is likely to prevent your opponents finding their eight-card heart fit. Being aware that you may only hold three-card support, partner will never bid on in his suit after a 1H-2H or 1S-2S sequence without five or more in his hand.

With 17/18pts, he can re-bid 2NT; with 19/20pts, 3NT.

If you do respond 1NT, opener should never re-bid his suit without six cards.

In response to an opening bid of 1H, which is far more likely to be a four-card suit, you should still be keen to raise with three-card support, except if your hand is completely flat, such as the one below:

♠ QJ2
♥ 863
♦ QJ2
♣ J762

Here, 1NT looks better. With 10 losers (see Tip 32), and no ruffing values, 2H is unlikely to be the best spot. Your hand also contains Queens and Jacks: these are cards likely to be useful in NTs, but less valuable in a suit contract (see Tip 12).

38 / AFTER AN INTERVENING TAKE-OUT DOUBLE, SUPPORT PARTNER AT LEAST ONE LEVEL HIGHER THAN USUAL

This is another area where you can improve your competitiveness.

When an opponent makes a take-out double of your partner's opening bid and you hold support for partner, this means that your opponents definitely hold a fit in another suit. The purpose of raising partner's suit pre-emptively, therefore, is to make life harder for the opponents to find that fit at the correct level.

Assume that partner has opened 1H, and your RHO now doubles. These are the three types of hand on which you will make a special bid:

a	b	c
♠ 642	♠ 32	♠ A42
♥ Q982	♥ KJ43	♥ KJ73
♦ Q854	♦ KJ109	♦ 9754
♣ 92	♣ 863	♣ K4

a) You would have passed your partner's 1H opening, but here you should raise to 2H. This is unlikely to prevent the opposition from finding their fit, but it has used up one level of bidding space. The bid should promise four-card support, allowing partner to compete further if he wishes.
b) You would normally have raised to 2H, so here you bid 3H. This raise is more effective at shutting out the opposition. With more shape, think about raising to 4H directly.
c) Here, you must indicate that you are not barraging, but hold a strong hand. The conventional response of 2NT tells partner that you would have raised to at least 3H. If partner is minimum, he re-bids 3H, if stronger 4H.

Without support for partner: respond 1NT with 6–9pts (promising two- or three-card support for partner's suit), or Redouble with 10pts or more. You can bid your own suit naturally with 6–9pts, but be aware that the doubler is likely to hold four cards in your suit.

As with all competitive situations, the more you can bully the opposition, the more likely it is that they will err from the correct path. Don't let them relax for a moment.

39 / DOUBLING OPPONENTS' NO-TRUMP CONTRACT ASKS PARTNER TO LEAD DUMMY'S FIRST BID SUIT

You should never double a 2NT or 3NT contract because you hold a strong hand. Your action may provide declarer with the information he needs to make his contract and, besides, because NT bidding is usually a matter of simple arithmetic, your opponents are unlikely to have misjudged their level too badly.

A double of a NT contract is lead directing because, if your partner can lead what you want, you are optimistic that you will defeat your opponents.

There are two types of lead directing double in this situation. The first is when your opponents' auction includes suit bids; the other is when only NTs have been bid (see Tip 40).

If your side has bid at all, most people agree that a double confirms that you wish to have your suit led.

When your opponents bid suits and end in 2NT or 3NT, a double asks partner to lead dummy's first bid suit.

The experts bid this hand identically in the big-money Cavendish Invitation Pairs in New York. Most found themselves doubled, and subsequently down …

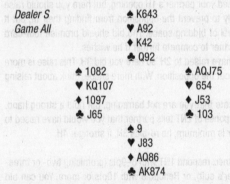

```
Dealer S          ♠ K643
Game All          ♥ A92
                  ♦ K42
                  ♣ Q92
      ♠ 1082              ♠ AQJ75
      ♥ KQ107             ♥ 654
      ♦ 1097              ♦ J53
      ♣ J65               ♣ 103
                  ♠ 9
                  ♥ J83
                  ♦ AQ86
                  ♣ AK874
```

South opened 1C and, over North's 1S response, re-bid 1NT. North raised to 2NT, and South bid 3NT confidently. East doubled, and now West had to find a lead.

When partner has made a lead-directing double, it is generally correct to lead the highest card in that suit, so that any values in dummy will be sandwiched between your card and partner's goodies. In this case, it proved vital to lead the top card.

When West led 10♠, dummy and East ducked, and South's singleton 9♠ dropped. Now, West's 8♠ had become significant, and was duly led. Again, both dummy and East ducked, and 8♠ held the trick. When West now led his final spade, either card from dummy lost, and East cashed his remaining spades to defeat the contract by one.

If West had not led his 10♠, East would have had to win the first trick, and West could not have been got on lead again to push another spade through until N/S had made ten tricks.

East's double looked risky, but it did not matter that he was otherwise so weak – this merely meant that partner had some useful values elsewhere.

The double was a particularly good bet here, because the descriptive bidding had marked N/S as only just strong enough for Game. Direct jumps to 3NT are sometimes made on far stronger hands than minimums. Here, however, it was pretty clear that N/S did not hold in excess of 26pts.

40 / DOUBLING OPPONENT'S NO-TRUMP AUCTION ASKS PARTNER TO MAKE AN UNUSUAL LEAD

When the opponents play in a NT contract after an auction which has contained only NT bids, a double of the final contract asks partner to make an unusual lead. I remember making a doubled contract in these circumstances against a pair I had not met before. Whilst we were totting up two doubled vulnerable overtricks, our opponents had this pleasant conversation:

RHO: 'But partner, my double asked you for an unusual lead. You just led top of a sequence.'

LHO: 'Well, that's pretty unusual for me ...'

When your opponents bid 1NT-3NT, neither will hold a five-card major suit, and the responder, having failed to use Stayman, is unlikely to have a four-card major suit. So, defensively, your thoughts should be on the major suits.

Reasonably often, when you play in a NT contract, you will have unconvincing cards in one suit. Thankfully, opponents do not always lead that suit, and you get home by making enough tricks in the other suits. So that your future opponents don't get away with this against you, it is important to know the meaning of a double after a purely NT auction: it asks partner to lead his shorter major suit.

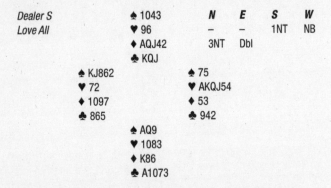

East's double asks West to lead his shorter major suit. On 7♥ lead, N/S go two down; on any other lead, they make 10 tricks.

Years ago, when I was braving the higher-stake Rubber bridge games for the first time, my partner doubled in exactly this situation. I led a minor suit, and my partner's face went redder and redder the more doubled overtricks the declarer made.

'I think,' she pronounced, like a James Bond villainess, 'you should return to the beginners' tables where you belong.'

For a change, I felt confident in my actions, and replied nonchalantly: 'Or, even better, next time I won't have a void in the suit you want me to lead!'

41 / A DOUBLE OF THE OPPONENT'S CONVENTIONAL BID SHOWS THAT SUIT

Whenever the opposition use a bid with an artificial meaning, you have the opportunity to show that suit by doubling. For example:

West	N	E	S	W
♠ 943	1NT	NB	2C	**Dbl**
♥ 952				
♦ K3				
♣ KQJ96				

West's double of South's Stayman response shows a good five-card club suit. The message you impart is like an overcall: a five- or six-card suit; asking partner to support you, or to lead your suit if the opponents play.

The same double could be used over on a 2C opening bid and 2D response; a Transfer bid, or any low-level artificial bid.

To double a high-level artificial bid is lead-directing, and is sometimes made on a void. However, ensure that it is your partner who will be on lead; otherwise you give your opponents useful information, which may help them to bid and play more accurately.

West	N	E	S	W
♠ 432	2H	NB	3H	NB
♥ 92	4NT	NB	5D	**Dbl**
♦ KQ73				
♣ A986				

With North having bid both hearts and no-trumps first, he is bound to be declarer, with your partner on lead. Doubling the 5D response requests that partner lead a diamond – surely best for you – against the final contract.

When the opponents use transfers, you have a choice of bids. If you double the transfer bid, it shows that you hold the bid suit (as with Stayman). If you bid the suit which they are showing by the transfer, you are making a take-out double of the suit they are showing.

42 / USE AN 'UNASSUMING CUE-BID' TO DISCOVER MORE ABOUT YOUR PARTNER'S HAND

During a contested auction, you often want to convey to partner that you like what you are hearing, but you are not sure what to say next. If the opposition has been silent, you can use Fourth Suit Forcing (see Tip 31), but in a competitive auction, you still have a good option: to bid their suit. This is generically known as an 'Unassuming Cue-bid' (UCB) – so called, because partner should not assume anything about your holding in the suit you have cue-bid. You may hold the Ace, or you may hold three small cards. The only significance of the bid is that you want to know more.

The most useful time to use a UCB is in response to your partner's overcall, when you hold a strong hand:

West	N	E	S	W
♠ J43	1H	1S	NB	**2H**
♥ 972				
♦ AK				
♣ A9832				

West cannot simply raise partner's overcall, as that would be a weak action. 2H is a UCB, informing partner that he holds three-card spade support or better and 11pts or more. If East is minimum 2S may be high enough whereas, if East has extra values, 4S Game is quite possible.

When you hold 11pts+ with support for partner's overcall, you **must** first make a UCB.

The bid is also useful in response to a take-out double:

West	N	E	S	W
♠ AJ43	1D	Dbl	NB	**2D**
♥ AJ43				
♦ 852				
♣ Q7				

You know that 4H or 4S must be making – but with which suit as trumps? To use an Unassuming Cue-bid tells partner that your two major suits are similar length and quality, and you want him to choose between them. This way, you will always get to play in an eight-card fit.

43 / IN RESPONSE TO PARTNER'S TAKE-OUT DOUBLE, BID TO THE FULL STRENGTH OF YOUR COMBINED HANDS

A take-out double is one of the most powerful and flexible bids in bridge. Yet, so often, its strength is undermined by poor responses. For social and club bridge, responding to your partner's double is straightforward once you know how.

The first thing, as always, is to translate what your partner is showing you before deciding what to bid yourself. For the sake of ease, you should imagine that your partner holds 13pts, and four-card support for each of the unbid suits (he has *promised* a minimum of three-card support in every suit). Then, bid as many of your best suit as you think your side can make, based on the combined values of your hands.

West		N	E	S	W
♠ A9843		1H	Dbl	NB	4S
♥ 972					
♦ AK3					
♣ Q9					

4S is correct because partner's double has promised an opening hand, and support for all suits other than hearts. Don't believe that you can bid 1S or 2S to 'see what partner might say next'. Partner has described his hand already; it is up to you to choose the level and suit. Remember that if you had this shape of hand with no points at all, you would still have had to respond 1S. So, it is vital that you bid up to the full strength of your hand.

The doubler must remain alert to the bid meanings as well:

West		N	E	S	W
♠ A432		–	–	1D	Dbl
♥ KQJ6		NB	2S	NB	?
♦ 3					
♣ K962					

What's the correct bid now? Pass.

This may come as a shock, but remember that West has assumed that you have exactly this hand (13pts, 4-4-4-1 shape), and he has decided that 2H is high enough. If he had wanted to be in Game opposite your hand, he was the one who should have bid it. Unless the doubler holds substantially more than 13pts, he should pass whatever you respond (unless you make a UCB – see Tip 42).

44 / WITH 6–10PTS, RESPOND WITH YOUR FOUR-CARD MAJOR IN RESPONSE BEFORE ANYTHING ELSE

If one hand has a shortage, a 4-4 major suit is often your best spot. For this reason, responder's priority is to show a four-card major suit at the 1-level before responding no-trumps and, with 6–10pts, even before showing a five- or six-card minor suit.

The reason is that with less than 10pts you are only worth one bid if your partner makes a minimum re-bid. Unless you show your major suit immediately, you may lose the chance to show it at all. Take this hand, from The Macallan Club Teams Championship:

Dealer South	♠ K1096		N	E	S	W
N/S Game	♥ 98		–	–	1D	NB
	♦ K8		1S	NB	3S	NB
	♣ K9864		4S			

	♠ 875		♠ A2
	♥ AQ1075		♥ KJ64
	♦ 96		♦ 7532
	♣ 1073		♣ QJ2

	♠ QJ43
	♥ 32
	♦ AQJ104
	♣ A5

The results on this hand were divided between those who knew this element of bidding, and those who did not. The former group reached 4S by the sequence shown; the latter bid: 1D-2C-2D-NB.

This second sequence is modest, but both South's 2D re-bid (a 2S re-bid would have been a reverse, promising 16pts+) and North's subsequent pass are eminently sensible.

With 11pts or more, responder can bid his suits naturally, having enough strength to bid the four-card major on the second round of bidding.

West	East	W	E
♠ AJ82	♠ KQ54	1H	2D
♥ AK73	♥ J3	2NT	3S
♦ 43	♦ KQJ87	**4S**	
♣ A32	♣ 86		

With 12pts, East is strong enough to bid his five-card minor suit, and then follow with his four-card spade suit. This describes his distribution correctly, and gets his side into the superior 4S contract. Had East held this hand but with only, say, 8pts, he should first respond 1S, ensuring that the 4-4 fit is not lost.

45 / IF YOUR TARGET IS GAME, BID BAD SUITS; IF YOUR TARGET IS SLAM, BID GOOD SUITS

This advice may seem a little peculiar to the uninitiated. However, there are very good tactical reasons to bid poor-quality suits.

The distinction between Game and Slam contracts is an important one. A partnership often reaches a Game contract because they hold the right values and a mildly suitable distribution. In these circumstances, a lead-deterring bid often gives you a vital edge in thin contracts. Slam bidding, however, must be more accurate, because the final contract is likely to be more precarious and imparting sound information to partner will prove more beneficial than trying to swizzle your opponents.

♠ J3
♥ AQ2
♦ KQJ9
♣ 9632

Your partner opens 1S. What should you respond? Since 3NT looks the most likely contract, to inhibit a club lead, responding 2C looks best. Often 3NT can be defeated if your opponents find the right lead, so it is your duty to try to confuse them.

♠ J6
♥ 952
♦ AQJ63
♣ AKQ

Partner opens 1D. Here, a Slam is quite possible and whether you favour a simple change of suit or a jump-shift, your response is best made in clubs. This way, your partner will worry less when he holds two or three small clubs, than if you had made a 'tactical' bid of hearts or spades.

There is another factor at work here: when you have to bid a short suit, it is wise to pick one lower-ranking than the suit for which you plan to subsequently show support, or one for which partner cannot have four-card support.

46 / YOUR HAND IMPROVES IF YOU HOLD LENGTH IN THE SUIT BID ON YOUR RIGHT, OR SHORTAGE IN A SUIT BID ON YOUR LEFT

Many players believe that the ideal time to overcall is when they hold a shortage in the suit their RHO has just opened; this isn't really the case.

♠ Q43
♥ AQJ87
♦ 7
♣ J863

Your opponent opens 1D. It's fine to overcall 1H. However, the hand won't necessarily play all that well in hearts: your opponents will lead diamonds, and you will be forced to trump in your own hand early on; if this happens repeatedly, your trumps may be so shortened that you lose control of the hand.

♠ Q43
♥ AQJ87
♦ J863
♣ 7

An overcall of 1H over an opening 1D looks a great deal better here. If your opponents lead diamonds, you can ruff them with dummy's trumps, preserving your own trump length to draw trumps and retain control of the hand.

Of course, the opponents may not lead diamonds, or dummy may not have enough trumps, but this is a basic principle you should have in the back of your mind.

This was a hand from an exciting semi-final of The Devonshire Cup a few years back:

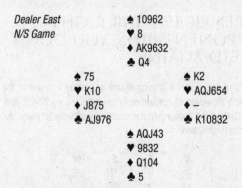

Dealer East
N/S Game

```
                        ♠ 10962
                        ♥ 8
                        ♦ AK9632
                        ♣ Q4
        ♠ 75                            ♠ K2
        ♥ K10                           ♥ AQJ654
        ♦ J875                          ♦ –
        ♣ AJ976                         ♣ K10832
                        ♠ AQJ43
                        ♥ 9832
                        ♦ Q104
                        ♣ 5
```

Jon Wilson, sitting East, opened 1H, and I overcalled 1S on the South cards, pleased to be holding length in the opener's suit. West responded 2C, and Peter Hardyment in the North seat now bid 4D (a 'fit-jump' which showed spade support and a good diamond suit). When East then bid 5C, I felt that the double fit, length in my RHO's suit and shortage in my LHO's suit bid, meant that this was a hand we should be playing. Despite the adverse vulnerability, I bid 5S, expecting to fail by a trick. West doubled and led A♣, K♥ and 10♥, missing the possible diamond ruff. As a result, my 'sacrifice' made, and the resulting swing proved crucial, as at the other table our team-mates played in 5C, making all 13 tricks on A♦ lead.

47 / AS OPENER, IF YOUR RIGHT-HAND OPPONENT BIDS, YOU DON'T HAVE TO BID AGAIN

To make an opener's re-bid – after a change of suit by partner – is one of the first lessons in bidding. However, this assumes an uncontested auction. If your right-hand opponent bids, if the auction is not proceeding positively for your side, pass may well be your best option.

South	N	E	S	W
♠ 2	–	–	1H	NB
♥ AJ852	1S	2C	?	
♦ KJ32				
♣ A63				

Most players blithely re-bid 2D, just as they had planned from the outset. However, your opponent's overcall has provided you with extra information and two additional bids: pass and double.

The information is that East holds an opening hand with good clubs and, more importantly, that so far the hand is a misfit. As discussed in the very first tip, if the hand is a misfit, you want to be defending.

The correct bid for South here is undoubtedly 'pass'. If North holds three-card heart support, he can show it on this round; if he has a strong hand, he can bid a new suit or his opponent's suit. The key point is that you have not encouraged him, or got him over-excited.

When you open the bidding and subsequently pass – as here – you guarantee a five-card suit. This is because if you held 12–14pts with a four-card suit, you would have opened 1NT; if you hold 15pts or more in this position, you should consider saying 'double'. The double in this position tells your partner that your side holds the majority of points, but that you lack a fit.

South	N	E	S	W
♠ Q2	–	–	1H	NB
♥ AJ85	1S	2C	**Dbl**	
♦ KQ98				
♣ A63				

This opener's re-bid of double says, in effect, that you were planning to re-bid at least 1NT, but that your opponent has made this impossible, either by bidding at too high a level, or because your hand does not contain the required two stoppers in your opponent's overcalled suit. Your partner can now bid on accordingly or, in the case of holding four clubs, pass for penalties.

Therefore, if you do keep bidding after an intervention from your right-hand opponent, your partner can expect you to be stronger than a minimum opener, with tolerance for his suit. If you re-bid no-trumps, partner can count on you to control the opponent's suit with two stoppers.

These simple understandings will increase your partnership confidence and accuracy, and avoid any unnecessary bidding risks.

A simple little tip to remind you that when bidding, space-saving bidding always provides the best chance of finding the best contract and that jumping should always show a fit, or extra distribution.

South	N	E	S	W
♠ AQJ9	–	–	1C	NB
♥ A2	1H	NB	?	
♦ 32				
♣ AKJ63				

Many players would now jump in spades, but there is no need. All possible Games and Slams are still available and 1S is 100% forcing. This leaves plenty of room for partner to re-bid to describe his hand further, or to use Fourth Suit Forcing to elicit further information from you. To jump here would simply waste your own side's bidding space and make reaching the correct contract more difficult.

When you do jump in a new suit, it should be to show extra distribution.

South	N	E	S	W
♠ J3	–	–	1H	NB
♥ AKJ752	1S	NB	?	
♦ AQJ84				
♣ –				

Here, South can re-bid 3D, guaranteeing 5-5 or 6-5 distribution and forcing partner to Game. Other jumps opposite partner's opening bids and responses can be played as 'Splinters'.

By the way, for social bridge players, brought up on old-fashioned bidding, learnt at their grandmother's knee, there is no need to jump in response to an opening bid just because you hold a strong hand.

South	N	E	S	W
♠ AJ964	–	1D	NB	?
♥ AK74				
♦ 4				
♣ A63				

Tempting as it may be to jump, you should not. You know that a Game contract is available, but you have a misfit with partner's suit. To change to suit to 1S is 100% forcing and allows partner to make the most descriptive bid in bridge: the opener's re-bid.

49 / DESCRIBING BIG TWO-SUITED HANDS

Describing two-suited hands remains the same whether you open the bidding at the 1-level, or start the auction with 2C – or some other forcing bid – and describe your shape subsequently.

All your bids should be made on the almost universal premise that you always open the longer of two suits first, and the higher ranking of two five-card suits, or two six-card suits, except with clubs and spades – when it is far more economical to open 1C first.

On this basis, you will find it easy to describe your hand, or decipher partner's distribution, even from quite complicated bidding sequences.

North		N	E	S	W
♠ AQ854		1D	NB	1H	NB
♥ 8		1S	NB	2H	NB
♦ AKJ863		?			
♣ 2					

You have shown 5-4 in diamonds and spades. Now you must show that you are actually 6-5. The way to do this is to re-bid your second suit. You bid 2S. This second spade bid promises a five-card suit and, therefore, you must hold *more* than five diamonds to have opened the bidding with 1D in the first place. Your minimum distribution of 6-5 is now confirmed, and partner is free to judge where to go from there.

As a general rule, when you hold a two-suited hand (5-5 or longer), you bid your first suit only once and re-bid your second suit to show extra length there and, by definition, greater length in your first suit.

The late, great Rixi Markus was far from pleased to be playing in the 'second best' contract on this deal:

Rixi (W)	Offender (E)	N	E	S	W
♠ –	♠ AQ7432	–	1S	NB	2C
♥ AJ9	♥ 83	NB	2D	NB	4C
♦ Q98	♦ AKJ103	NB	4S	all pass	
♣ AK98762	♣ –				

East's failure to re-bid diamonds left him with a scramble to make 4S, whereas had he bid his diamonds a second time, the Slam in that denomination would have been easy to find.

Not unusually, Rixi's partner came out worse in the post-mortem: glasses cracked, plaster fell from the ceiling, dogs ran away with tails between legs – and he never got a word in!

50 / BE PREPARED TO RE-BID NO-TRUMPS WITH A SINGLETON IN PARTNER'S SUIT

This is something for which you must be prepared when you hold a 4-4-4-1 hand and partner responds in your singleton. However, on the far more common 5-4-3-1 hands, a no-trump re-bid is still sometimes best. Take a look at this hand:

South	N	E	S	W
♠ AQ8			1D	NB
♥ 8	1H	NB	?	
♦ AJ863				
♣ KJ94				

Here, your choice lies between re-bidding 2C or 1NT. The advantage of the latter is that it protects your holdings in spades and clubs against the likely opening lead. Since 3NT is far more likely to be the best final Game contract (opposed to 5C or 5D), it makes sense for you to propose playing it, without giving away too much information to your opponents.

South	N	E	S	W
♠ K6	–	–	1C	NB
♥ 4	1H	NB	?	
♦ A63				
♣ AKQJ753				

Here, you might have opened with some kind of Strong Two, although there are plenty of sound reasons to begin at the 1-level. However, once partner bids hearts, the re-bid of 3NT seems marked. If partner counts you for 19–20pts and a balanced hand, he is unlikely to be disappointed by your eight-and-a-half trick hand. If he is relatively weak, you will still have excellent chances of scoring Game.

South	N	E	S	W
♠ A9854	–	–	1S	NB
♥ A53	2C	NB	?	
♦ AKJ8				
♣ 2				

On this hand, your re-bid should definitely **not** re-bid 1NT (or 2NT). Firstly, your hand consists largely of Aces and Kings, which suggests that a trump contract may play well. Secondly, your 2D re-bid allows partner to move towards no-trumps if he has something in hearts, but stay away from the no-trump contract with nothing in hearts – and that is about right.

51 / LISTEN TO WHAT YOUR OPPONENTS HAVE BID AND COUNT THE HAND

When dummy hits baize, do as the experts do – take your time. Form an overview of the situation so that you will be ready to face the challenges as they arise.

Count your winners or loser (see Tip 61) and analyse the lead (see Tips 53–5). If either opponent has bid, remind yourself of the auction and, importantly, add up your combined point-count, and work out how many points your opposition hold. You will be surprised at how often you are able to place the remaining cards, either immediately, or quite shortly into the play of the hand.

An opening bid of 1NT is particularly revealing, disclosing as it does a balanced distribution and an exact point-count.

This deal illustrates the value of remembering the auction, and counting the hand:

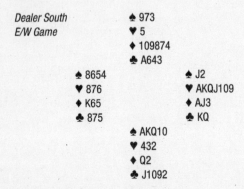

Because N/S were playing transfers, North had to pass 1NT (rather than making a Weak Take-out). East doubled, hoping to extract a sizeable penalty but, when North ran to 2D, he decided to have a punt at 4H. South led A♠, and declarer took stock.

He had three certain losers: two spades, and A♣. The contract therefore depends on not losing a diamond. An unthinking declarer takes the diamond finesse through North – the only way he could finesse – and, anyway, North bid diamonds. Such an unthinking effort would receive its just result. Instead take pleasure from detection and deduction …

South cashes ♠AK, and continues with Q♠. East trumps this, and pulls trumps. He now plays K♣ and, when this loses to North's A♣, he knows the whole picture. E/W hold 24pts between them, leaving N/S with 16pts. South must hold 12pts for his 1NT opener, so North's A♣ is his only card of value.

Q♦ is unquestionably with South. As no finesse position exists, when North correctly returns a club, East should cash ♦AK, and play for Q♦ to drop. It does – and you have brought home an 'unmakable' contract.

Don't, whatever you do, lead J♦ thinking this is a finesse. South merely covers this with his Q♦ and, once K♦ is played, and A♦ cashed, you are left with a small diamond in each hand. You can only lead a high card for a finesse if you (or dummy) hold the card beneath it.

If, on the hand above, South had shown up with A♣ as well as his ♠AKQ, you would then have known that North holds Q♦. He must do, for South has shown 13pts, and cannot hold a further 2pts and still have opened a Weak NT (12–14pts).

52 / LISTEN TO WHAT YOUR OPPONENTS HAVE NOT BID AND COUNT THE HAND

For all the reasons we have seen in the previous tip, you should be alert to inferences you can take from an uncontested auction – although they are often much harder to spot.

An old friend of mine, Adrian Palmer, spotted the right line on this hand only just in time, when we were playing in the Sobranie Championship Final many years ago:

			N	E	S	W
Dealer West	♠ AK1098					
Love All	♥ 853		–	–	–	1H
	♦ 1042		NB	2C	NB	2NT
	♣ 105		NB	3H	NB	**4H**

♠ J54		♠ Q62
♥ J10974		♥ AQ2
♦ AK5		♦ Q96
♣ AK		♣ Q842

♠ 73
♥ K6
♦ J873
♣ J9763

Adrian opened 1H and, after his NT re-bid, I doubtfully showed him three-card support. He raised to 4H which, since 3NT failed at the other table, was a smart move.

North led ♠AK, and then a third spade, which South ruffed with 6♥. South then exited with 3♣. The contract now depends upon not losing a trump trick and it seemed to Adrian, just as it would to any of us, that the heart finesse was the only available play. However, as I watched, feigning disinterest, Adrian led J♥, and opened his mouth to call for a card from dummy. At this point he stopped. As he explained to me later, it suddenly occurred to him that **North had started with ♠AK1098 and that, had he held K♥ as well, he would certainly have overcalled 1S**. As the North player had appeared anything but backward in the bidding on the previous hands, Adrian now placed K♥ with South and called for A♥ from dummy. The K♥ fell politely.

At the time, we were at the top table, and there were several kibitzers watching South, one of whom was British International Jeremy Flint. The kibitzers seemed to think Adrian's play was suspect … Had he seen his opponent's hand? Jeremy Flint merely nodded at him, said, 'Quite right,' and started jotting down the hand for his newspaper column.

53 / ANALYSE THE LEAD (1): IS ANOTHER SUIT MORE DANGEROUS?

This should be part of your thinking every time dummy goes down. Apart from anything else, remembering the opening lead is often important when making a complicated decision 10 tricks later.

In suit contracts there is always the concern of singleton or doubleton leads, and of whether or not the leader holds an honour. In NT contracts, those who find the Rule of 11 useful may use it to place the outstanding high cards in the suit but, often, the quantity of cards is more useful knowledge than the quality. This next hand is typical of a type which defeats even quite experienced players:

Dealer N	♠ A876		*N*	*E*	*S*	*W*
Love All	♥ 872		NB	NB	1NT	NB
	♦ 1042		**3NT**			
	♣ KJ10					

	♠ 542		♠ KQ109
	♥ Q1053		♥ KJ2
	♦ A53		♦ 76
	♣ 852		♣ 7643

	♠ J3
	♥ A96
	♦ KQJ98
	♣ AQ4

North's raise to 3NT opposite the Strong NT opener is frisky – the two 10s are nice – but at Rubber bridge any sniff of a Game is worth following.

West leads 3♥, and South plans. With only one stopper in hearts, it is standard to hold up A♥ for at least one round, but see what happens if you do that here. East wins, switches to K♠. Do you hold up there too? You do and East switches back to hearts. Now, you'll lose a spade, three heart tricks, and A♦, for one off.

Back to trick 1…

Before ducking the first trick, ask yourself a key question: is there another suit you fear even more than the one led? You should be as afraid of spades as you are of hearts, and you cannot afford for the opposition to hop back and forth between them collecting tricks whilst you work out when to take your Aces.

The solution lies in West's 3♥ lead. If E/W are playing fourth highest leads (you can ask them if you are not sure), this card marks West with only a four-card heart suit. You know this because dummy contains 2♥, and therefore West cannot hold a lower card than 3♥. On that basis, you can win trick 1, dislodge A♦, lose three more heart tricks, and then claim the remaining tricks for your contract.

54 / ANALYSE THE LEAD (2): WHY HAVE THEY NOT LED THEIR SUIT?

If I have time before the opening lead, I like to anticipate what suit my opponent will lead. If you are aware of normal leads in certain situations, you can draw winning conclusions from an unexpected play. The most usual explanation for an unexpected lead is a singleton.

This hand should have been made by the experienced declarer, but in one Chicago bridge game, to my surprise, it was not.

Dealer East	♠ 974		**N**	**E**	**S**	**W**
N/S Game	♥ Q74		–	NB	1H	1S
	♦ 10842		2H	2S	**4H**	
	♣ AJ2					

♠ AQJ105		♠ K86
♥ 1053		♥ J2
♦ J953		♦ 76
♣ 3		♣ K107654

	♠ 32	
	♥ AK986	
	♦ AKQ	
	♣ Q98	

South might expect E/W to attack spades from the outset, but West led 3♣ and, after a little thought, declarer played low from dummy. East won with K♣, returned 10♣ for West to ruff, and then E/W cashed ♠AK, allowing East to give West another ruff. Two down.

It's unfortunate that East held a concealed six-card club suit and, as West had overcalled, it was slightly more likely that he held K♣ than East. However, South can afford one club loser; to risk adverse ruffs was careless. West's unexpected lead should be the clincher. South must ask himself: would West lead away from ♣Kxx or ♣Kxxx, when his side have bid and supported spades?

55 / ANALYSE THE LEAD (3): COUNTING THE HANDS FROM THE OPENING LEAD

As discussed in the previous tip, failure by the opponents to lead their bid and agreed suit should alert you to possible dangers – and potential information. The simple inference to draw from an unusual lead is that your opponent has either:

- found a better lead – a singleton, for example, or
- found that leading his own suit makes him uncomfortable; for example, being reluctant – quite rightly – to lead a suit headed by AQ or AJ.

If your opponent does not lead Ace or King of his suit, then he does not hold any suit headed by AK; if he does not lead an honour, his hand is unlikely to contain any sequence.

This may sound obvious to you, but the deductions you can then draw about the hand will give you a huge advantage as declarer, and keep your hair from turning grey or, in my case, from falling out …

Take this interesting deal from a multiple teams event:

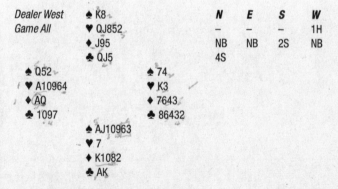

South's 2S overcall showed a very strong hand with six spades. 4S is a decent spot, although 3NT is less stressful.

West led 10♣, N/S hold 25pts between them, so West, as opener, must hold most of the outstanding 15pts. South looked very likely to lose two diamonds and a heart, and therefore had to avoid losing a trump trick. Obviously, West was more likely to hold Q♠ than East, but was there any way declarer could uncover further evidence before committing himself to the finesse?

As you might suspect – or indeed work out – the clue was in the opening lead. South might have been expecting a heart lead, but instead received 10♣. Whilst this could have been a singleton, the resultant seven-card club suit East would have to hold might have caused him to make a bid. In any case, when in doubt, it is sensible to play for the distribution to be relatively flat. You should therefore deduce that as West has failed to lead a top heart, he cannot hold ♥AK. So, if East holds, say, K♥, then West must hold every other high card to justify his opening bid. For this reason, you should place Q♠ with West, and lead a little spade and, when West plays low, finesse with dummy's 8♠.

Whether the declarer I watched had any of these thoughts passing through his mind, I am not certain, but he looked remarkably calm when he took the spade finesse at trick 2. In my experience, this is a sign of great knowledge in a bridge player – or blissful ignorance.

56 / RULE OF 7

In the long run, it is vital to know the reason behind any course of action, so that you can adapt your knowledge to cope with imperfect situations. I am not a fan of flow-charts or flippers, pigeon-holing everything into little rules, but this Rule of 7 is useful to have in the back of your mind.

The rule concerns the number of times you should withhold your high card when a suit you are worried about is led against your NT contract.

The purpose of a hold-up in NTs is to attempt to exhaust one opponent (usually the partner of the leader) of his supply of the suit, so that he, at least, cannot return the danger suit. In other words, you are trying to cut communications between your opponents. In general, this action is only necessary when the danger suit is splitting badly for, if it is behaving, it often can't produce enough tricks to defeat you. The Rule of 7 helps you to judge how many times you should hold up to achieve your objective.

Let's take the suit led in isolation to demonstrate the point:

In (a) 5♠ is led, and RHO plays Q♠. How many times should you hold up your A♠? The Rule of 7 states that you should add up the total number of cards in the danger suit held by you and dummy, and subtract this total from seven. The result is the number of times you should not play your Ace. Here, the rule suggests that, with five cards between you, you should not play your A♠ twice (7 − 5 = **2**), winning only on the final round. As you can see, that would serve to exhaust RHO of his supply of the suit. If the division had been 4-4, it would have been impossible to sever communications.

In (b) RHO overtakes Q♠ with A♠, and returns 5♠. With six cards in the suit, the rule suggests withholding your high card only one time, which you have already done by losing the first trick. You therefore win the second trick with K♠. Again, this exhausts RHO of spades. If the suit had divided 4-3, RHO would still hold a spade but, usually, an even break does not threaten you. If, on a particular hand, you judge that it will, you can hold up for a further round.

An opponent, once exhausted of the suit, can be allowed on lead safely whilst the player with remaining cards can be kept off lead (see Tip 57). This increases your chances to make difficult contracts.

It is just as dangerous to hold up for too long as it is not to hold up at all. Once opponents have made a couple of tricks in one suit, they may switch to another. By this time, you may have lost the vital 'tempo' required to win the race setting up your extra tricks.

57 / AVOIDANCE (1): IF ONE OPPONENT IS A DANGER TO YOU, KEEP HIM OFF LEAD AT ALL COSTS

The art of identifying a dangerous opponent and keeping him off lead is known as 'avoidance', and can provide you with a huge edge over the opposition. The need for avoidance is usually at its greatest when playing in NTs.

Firstly, you have to identify the dangerous opponent:

a

♠ 97

♠ KJ853　　♠ Q104

♠ A62

b

♠ 94

♠ A10876　　♠ Q52

♠ KJ3

In (a) LHO leads 5♠, RHO plays Q♠, and you withhold your A♠ until the last round, in accordance with the Rule of 7 – see Tip 56. Clearly, when you finally win with A♠, the danger hand is LHO, as he has spade winners in his hand, whilst RHO is safe, because he has no more spades.

In (b) LHO leads 7♠, and RHO plays Q♠, which you win with K♠. It is now RHO who presents the danger, as he can lead a spade *through* your remaining holding of ♠J3 towards LHO's ♠A10xx. If LHO gains the lead, he cannot play another spade without the lead coming around to your J♠.

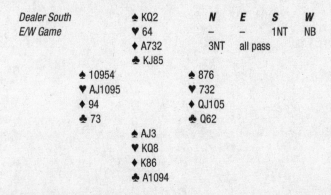

Dealer South	♠ KQ2	*N*	*E*	*S*	*W*
E/W Game	♥ 64	–	–	1NT	NB
	♦ A732	3NT	all pass		
	♣ KJ85				

♠ 10954　　♠ 876
♥ AJ1095　　♥ 732
♦ 94　　♦ QJ105
♣ 73　　♣ Q62

♠ AJ3
♥ KQ8
♦ K86
♣ A1094

If a danger hand holds an entry in an outside suit, whatever you do may not be enough. However, when a contract looks tough, optimism is the order of the day. In this example, your problem is only to identify the dangerous opponent; the avoidance itself is straightforward:

West leads J♥, North and East play small, and you win with Q♥. You now have six tricks outside clubs, so your target is a third trick there. Which opponent must be kept off lead? It's East, as if he wins a trick, he will return 8♠ through your ♥K8 and into West's ♥A109x, and you will lose the next four tricks. So, when finessing in clubs, lead J♣ from dummy and, if East covers, win; if East plays low, you play low also. Even if West wins, your ♥ K8 is safe from attack from West.

What, you may ask, if East holds A♥? In that case, your K♥ is quite safe anyway, so your care may go unrewarded, but you will still make your contract. In fact, East won't hold A♥ because, if he had held it, he would have played it at trick 1.

58 / AVOIDANCE (2): DON'T FINESSE INTO THE DANGER HAND

I have had several opportunities to play against the legendary Rixi Markus; she was a truly formidable Rubber bridge opponent. However, it was she who first proved to me that even top players take their eye off the ball for a moment. I say this, because in the next example Rixi missed a play she would have considered obvious.

I (West) was playing in partnership with Pat Cotter (East) against Rixi (South) and Derek Rimington (North):

I led 6♥, and Pat won and returned a heart, which Rixi won at the second chance. She now cashed ♠AQ, and led a small diamond towards her hand. To my astonishment she played J♦, and I was able to win and cash the setting tricks. Derek leant over to peer at my hand, presumably to see how many diamonds I had held. No one spoke, and the next hand was dealt.

Dealer North	♠ AQ	*N*	*E*	*S*	*W*
N/S Game	♥ 852	1C	NB	1D	NB
	♦ 1074	2C	NB	**3NT**	
	♣ AK753				

♠ 1093	♠ J8765
♥ KJ964	♥ Q10
♦ Q3	♦ 952
♣ J108	♣ Q92

♠ K42
♥ A73
♦ AKJ86
♣ 64

Diamonds must be established to succeed, but West must not be permitted to gain the lead. Often, with eight cards missing the Queen, the finesse is correct. Here, however, to finesse into the danger hand is too great a risk, and the finesse should be spurned. Lay down ♦AK and hope that Q♦ is located either in the safe hand – in which case you can afford to lose the lead there later – or a singleton or doubleton in the danger hand, so that it falls, as it would have done on this occasion. If I had held ♦Qxx or ♦Qxxx, there would have been no play for the contract on these lines.

In this situation, when the card you were worried about turns up in the safe hand, and which you could have finessed, somebody will usually tell you that you squandered an overtrick. Take no notice. You know you made the right play; if your opponents don't get it, leave them in the dark.

59 / AVOIDANCE (3): STRAND THE SAFE OPPONENT ON LEAD

Avoidance play is so vital to success as declarer that it warrants a third tip devoted to a variation on standard avoidance technique. Here, you are reversing your usual tactic. Instead of preventing the danger hand from gaining the lead, you are stranding the safe hand on lead.

This hand demonstrates the solution to a taxing avoidance problem, variations of which crop up all the time. Once you know the expert secret, you'll find them a pleasure to play.

Dealer South	♠ AK98	N	E	S	W
N/S Game	♥ 42	–	–	1NT	NB
	♦ 6432				
	♣ AKJ	**3NT**			

	♠ J5		♠ Q1062
	♥ KJ952		♥ Q64
	♦ J108		♦ Q9
	♣ 952		♣ 7643

	♠ 743
	♥ A86
	♦ AK75
	♣ Q108

I first met this hand years ago in a Simultaneous Pairs event. Since then, it has remained a favourite of mine, and generations of students have faced its challenge.

West leads 5♥. With six tricks outside diamonds, you must develop three tricks from that suit. However, once you hold up A♥ twice, you know from the play of the cards that East holds no further hearts and is your safe hand, and West is dangerous. How can you establish the extra diamond trick without letting West gain the lead?

If you cash ♦A and/or K♦, East should throw Q♦ – trying to promote an entry in his partner's hand. If you play ♦AK5, West wins the third round. In fact, there is no way to keep West off lead, but there is a way to keep East *on* lead!

Cross to dummy with a club, and lead 2♦. When East plays small, win with A♦, and cross back to dummy. Now, lead 3♦; when East plays Q♦, duck, *stranding* him – the safe hand – on lead. West cannot be got on lead in any other suit, so you have now established your fourth diamond into a winner, and the ninth trick for your contract.

If East happens to hop up with Q♦ on the first round, duck then – the effect is the same.

Many no-trump contracts feature a danger and a safe hand; if you can identify them, you have a huge advantage. Avoidance situations occur in suit contracts also, but no-trumps is their prime territory.

60 / AS DECLARER, PLAY DECEPTIVELY

Bridge players often run to Backgammon and Poker, not because they are superior Games – though each has its charms – but because they get a longing to be their own boss. The unselfish nature of playing a partnership Game can sometimes become stressful. ('Sometimes'? – who am I kidding?) As declarer, however, you are completely in charge, and you should relish the one time when deceit can harm only your opponents, and utilise it to the full. (I have encountered too many dummies who have attempted to enhance their side's fortune through unethical behaviour. If you must chatter, fiddle with beads, wiggle your eyebrows, or clear your throat loudly, your behaviour will doubtless be acceptable in the nearest bar …)

Now, let's look at a couple of simple situations:

In (a) LHO leads 5♠ against a NT contract; RHO playing Q♠. It would be completely **wrong** for South to win this trick with A♠. It announces that he holds K♠ also. Why? Would you win trick one with ♠Axx. In a NT contract, almost always no; you would hold up. But with ♠Kxx you would have to immediately, or risk winning none at all.

In (b) you want to cross to dummy. Don't play 2♠ to A♠. This helps your opponents to count you for K♠. Instead, lead 8♠ to Q♠. Both opponents will wonder whether their partner holds K♠ and, by concealing 2♠, good players may misread their partner's signals.

These are small points, but they can swing Game contracts in your favour.

This next hand was featured as revolutionary in the 1960s. These days, a decent pair would smoke out the swindle with accurate signals but, back then, the declarer emerged victorious.

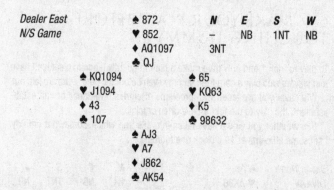

Dealer East	♠ 872		**N**	**E**	**S**	**W**
N/S Game	♥ 852		–	NB	1NT	NB
	♦ AQ1097		3NT			
	♣ QJ					

♠ KQ1094		♠ 65
♥ J1094		♥ KQ63
♦ 43		♦ K5
♣ 107		♣ 98632

	♠ AJ3
	♥ A7
	♦ J862
	♣ AK54

Following the Strong 1NT opening from South, North correctly raised to 3NT. When West led K♠, at one table, declarer ducked. West promptly switched to J♥, and the defence came to a spade, three hearts tricks, and K♦ for one off.

Our hero, at the second table, recognised the danger of a heart switch, and realised that if spades were 5-2, he only needed to hold up once and, if they were 4-3, he could afford to lose three spade tricks. He therefore dropped J♠ on the first trick! West, not unnaturally, assumed that declarer held ♠AJ doubleton, and led another spade enthusiastically. South won and took the diamond finesse; East won K♦, but had no spades left to return. Consequently, South emerged with 10 tricks.

61 / MAKE YOUR PLAN BEFORE TOUCHING DUMMY

To play to trick 1 and only then make a plan frequently leads to disaster. I have met players who play a card from dummy even before the other suits are laid out.

Whenever you are faced with problems of entries, avoidance or suit establishment, the play to the first trick is often crucial.

See whether you would have fallen into this trap which, somewhat unfairly, I set some students at 10 o'clock one morning ...

Dealer North	♠ A8			N	E	S	W
Love All	♥ AK86			1H	NB	1NT	NB
	♦ Q95			3NT			
	♣ AJ106						

	♠ Q10752		♠ 943
	♥ J105		♥ Q92
	♦ 64		♦ A73
	♣ K72		♣ Q983

	♠ KJ6
	♥ 743
	♦ KJ1082
	♣ 54

West leads 5♠. What card do you play from dummy? Take your time ... Because, if you play low, you will go down. E/W will hold up A♦ twice and you will be sealed off from the rest of your diamond winners.

Instead, retain K♠ as a certain entry to your hand by playing A♠ at trick 1. You may give up a spade trick, but you gain two extra diamond tricks – and that is the difference between making and failing in 3NT.

With a choice, preserve entries into your weaker hand and, as you will see in the following tip, into the hand with the long suit.

Take your time at the bridge table. Players who try to hurry you are doing so to distract you from giving the hand your best shot.

Whilst you can give any hand as much thought as you like, generally the best moment to spend time assessing your plan of action is before touching dummy.

If any other player, including dummy, plays a card from the exposed hand, smack their hand with a whip-like crack and exclaim in a scandalised tone: 'Don't touch my dummy!' Everyone will be so shocked, they'll never try to hurry you up again.

62 / RETAIN ENTRIES IN THE HAND WITH THE LONG SUIT YOU PLAN TO ESTABLISH

If you want to be a bridge player – a real bridge player – you have to love establishing long suits; it is the most effective way of creating extra tricks in both NT and suit contracts. The single most important element is to ensure that you have sufficient entries to play that suit repeatedly.

			N	E	S	W
Dealer South	♠ KQ					
E/W Game	♥ 642		–	–	1C	NB
	♦ AJ654		1D	NB	2NT	NB
	♣ 853		3NT			

♠ J1095		♠ 7432
♥ K73		♥ J1085
♦ Q1097		♦ K
♣ 107		♣ QJ92

♠ A86
♥ AQ9
♦ 853
♣ AK64

This is a hand from a local Swiss Teams competition final a few years back:

J♠ was led against South's 3NT. With six tricks outside diamonds, South's target was to make three tricks there. Entries to dummy are strained, with spades led already, so each remaining entry must be utilised. At trick 2, declarer played 3♦ and also low from dummy, East winning perforce with K♦. Another spade was returned, killing dummy's last outside entry. To secure the contract, there is now a simple play: lead a low diamond from dummy! If East wins; the rest of the suit is good; if East shows out – as he does – the finesse against West's ♦Q10 is marked. The key was not to part with A♦ until you were certain it was being used to best effect.

Ducking is generally a good way to maintain communications. Look at this simple example:

West	East
♠ AJ8	♠ 952
♥ AK72	♥ 93
♦ AKQ5	♦ 32
♣ 62	♣ AK8754

West opens 2NT and is raised to 3NT. 5♥ is led. West should win, and then play a low club from each hand. Now, whatever N/S play, he can win, play his other club to dummy's Ace and hope that the suit splits kindly. No other play offers any chance of success.

63 / LOOK OUT FOR THE LOSER-ON-LOSER PLAY

One of the most effective ways for defenders to attack declarer is by making him trump in his own hand, reducing his length in trumps, and forcing him out of control.

Another successful line might be for a defender to ruff a trick with a high trump, tempting declarer to over-ruff with a higher trump and promote a defensive trump trick (see Tip 78).

Thankfully, declarer often has a means of countering such an assault. Instead of parting with an unaffordable trump, or a high trump which might promote a trick for the defence, look for a potentially losing card in another suit to discard instead.

If you have reached the point where you have to make the rest of the tricks to succeed, you must imagine where the outstanding high cards must lie in order for you to have any chance of success. More often, you have the luxury of a little 'slack', and that must be used to your advantage …

Dealer East	♠ K75	**N**	**E**	**S**	**W**
Love All	♥ 9642	–	NB	1S	2D
	♦ J64	2S	NB	**4S**	
	♣ KQ3				

♠ J94		♠ 102
♥ K7		♥ J10853
♦ AKQ973		♦ 102
♣ 107		♣ 9865

	♠ AQ863
	♥ AQ
	♦ 85
	♣ AJ42

This well-known hand usually causes problems, but not for this experienced student. West led ♦AKQ, and on third round East decided to ruff with 10♠ – a fine use of an otherwise useless card.

After this first-rate defence, the contract lay in the hands of the declarer: if she over-ruffs with Q♠, she will promote West's J♠ into a trick, and go on to lose K♥.

Knowing that a finesse should always be counted as a loser, the declarer – Virginia Manch – was able to find the winning play. With seeming nonchalance, she tossed away Q♥. Now, whatever the defence got up to, she could not lose another trick.

'I knew it would be something like throwing away a King or a Queen,' Virginia concluded knowingly. The table stared at me, agreeing wholeheartedly what a tricky character I was.

64 / SAFEGUARD YOUR CONTRACT – LOOK FOR THE SAFETY PLAY

Building up banks of knowledge on which to call at moments of crisis is vital for long-term success at bridge. At Rubber bridge you have a simple target: your contract. Overtricks are of little value and, generally, you would never risk your contract for the chance of an extra trick. To this end, it is your duty to anticipate any bad breaks which may occur in the trump suit or in side suits.

The following examples (using, for purely arbitrary reasons, hearts as the suit) outline a few of the more important 'safety plays' – so called because, whilst sometimes costing one trick, they safeguard against the loss of two.

Between dummy and your own hand, you hold eight cards including ♥AK10. These cards may be in one hand, or in opposite hands. You are prepared to lose one trick, but not two. To this end, you should cash the honour on its own, and then lead a low card towards the honour and the 10, intending to play 10♥ if your opponent plays low. This holds the trick if LHO holds ♥QJxx (as in the example), and you then lose just one further trick. If LHO puts in an honour, you cover this and win, return to hand with another suit, and lead again towards 10♥.

If RHO wins the trick, the suit is 3-2, and you will win the third round with A♥ later.

If RHO holds ♥QJxx, you cannot avoid the loss of two tricks.

You hold nine cards, missing J♥, but not the important intermediates. The correct play here is to first cash an honour from the hand which contains two honours. This way, should either hand show out, you will be able to finesse the Jack successfully later.

```
             ♥ A1042
   ♥ J876                ♥ –
             ♥ KQ953
```

If you cash A♥, you can no longer avoid the loss of a trick to J♥.

Now, you need to take the above thinking one step further:

```
             ♥ A42
   ♥ –                  ♥ J1087
             ♥ KQ9653
```

Here, you hold nine cards between you, missing J♥ **and** 10♥. The key is that if the suit breaks 4-0, you will need two cards higher than the two you are missing to beat them. You must cash A♥ first and, if the suit divides as in the example, you can catch both J♥ and 10♥ between the ♥KQ and 9♥ in your own hand.

If LHO holds all four cards, you cannot avoid the loss of a trick.

Understanding the thinking behind these safety plays, you should be able to work out your action for other holdings. Inevitably, nearly every time you make the correct safety play at the table, the suit will split perfectly, and everyone will wonder why you took so long. However, when you succeed against a really horrendous break, you will see how rewarding the effort can be.

This hand, set for an invitational Teams of Four event, reveals how the correct thought, and subsequent technique, can make more than just one trick's difference. Everyone was in the aggressive 3NT contract, but only two declarers brought home the contract: the two most experienced players present. Would you get it right?

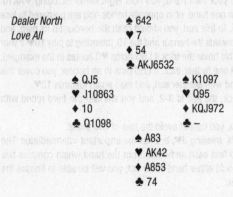

```
Dealer North          ♠ 642
Love All              ♥ 7
                      ♦ 54
                      ♣ AKJ6532

        ♠ QJ5                      ♠ K1097
        ♥ J10863                   ♥ Q95
        ♦ 10                       ♦ KQJ972
        ♣ Q1098                    ♣ —

                      ♠ A83
                      ♥ AK42
                      ♦ A853
                      ♣ 74
```

J♥ was led, and won with K♥. Declarer led 4♣ and, to preserve entries, played J♣ when West played low. Unfortunately, East showed out, and now declarer made only three club tricks – West still holding ♣Q109 – instead of the six he might have made had he contemplated a little more carefully.

If East holds all four clubs, the contract is doomed and, if the suit is 2-2 or 3-1, it is an easy make. The only distribution for which you can actively cater is for West to hold all four clubs. In that situation, if you duck in dummy whatever card West plays, you must score the remaining tricks. You return to hand later, and finesse against West's marked holding.

West could make the going more difficult for declarer: at my table, partner played 10♣ on the declarer's 4♣. Perhaps this contributed to South's mis-play of J♣ … but, in any case, it was a decent attempt to mislead declarer.

In fact, the correct play is for West to drop Q♣ on the first round; a well-known expert false-card: even experts miss it sometimes.

65 / PLANNING SUIT CONTRACTS (1): COUNT YOUR LOSERS

Counting your losers in each suit is often preferable to looking for winners in suit contracts, because it helps you to focus your mind on the real task facing you: to dispose of excess losers. Sometimes, you may want to count your total tricks as well, to double-check your thinking.

Always count finesses as losers. This way, you will not be disappointed when they fail, and you will seek alternatives to taking them (see Tip 68).

There are only two main ways of getting rid of losers: discarding them on dummy's long suit, and trumping them with dummy's trumps.

Once clear on this thinking, you will find it easier to spot the solutions to the tricky hands which sometimes trip up the hardiest of campaigners:

Dealer East	♠ J975	**N**	**E**	**S**	**W**
Love All	♥ K84	–	NB	1S	NB
	♦ KJ10	3NT	NB	**4S**	
	♣ KQ3				

♠ A4	♠ K2
♥ QJ102	♥ 976
♦ 973	♦ A8642
♣ 10975	♣ 864

♠ Q10863
♥ A53
♦ Q5
♣ AJ2

North's 3NT response is a 'Pudding Raise' (see Tip 103), the essential replacement to the outdated Delayed Game Raise.

Q♥ led. Declarer has two losers in spades, one heart, and one diamond loser. There are no shortages in dummy to provide ruffs. Is there a long suit? A long suit in dummy is merely one which contains more cards than there are in your own hand. Diamonds qualify. Here, declarer establishes this side suit immediately, because if he were to play on trumps first, the defenders would continue with hearts and score their trick on the third round. To this end, declarer wins trick one in hand, and plays Q♦ and 5♦ until East parts with his A♦. On the likely heart return, declarer wins in dummy and plays K♦ to discard a heart from hand. Only now can he start to pull the opponents' trumps.

66 / PLANNING SUIT CONTRACTS (2): IF YOU HAVE TOO MANY LOSERS, HESITATE BEFORE DRAWING TRUMPS

The moment you have few enough losers to make your contract, you should draw trumps as quickly as possible. If you hold too many losers, most often you should not pull trumps, as you may need dummy's for ruffing losers or as entries whilst establishing a long suit. If you can pull trumps and still leave sufficient entries to – or ruffs in – dummy, then draw those trumps fast.

In practice for teams of four, the two tables got the most from this intriguing deal. Drawing trumps was far from the thoughts of either declarer, who demonstrated the value of every little pip.

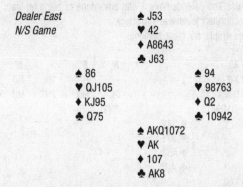

Dealer East
N/S Game

```
              ♠ J53
              ♥ 42
              ♦ A8643
              ♣ J63
  ♠ 86                    ♠ 94
  ♥ QJ105                 ♥ 98763
  ♦ KJ95                  ♦ Q2
  ♣ Q75                   ♣ 10942
              ♠ AKQ10072
              ♥ AK
              ♦ 107
              ♣ AK8
```

Everyone managed to bid 6S, and each declarer received Q♥ lead. To succeed, Q♣ must fall in two rounds or, by far the better chance, dummy's long diamond suit must be established to provide a club discard from hand. As so often with a very strong hand opposite a weak one, the main problem confronting the declarer is one of entries to dummy.

The best line is to play a low diamond from both hands first – keeping A♦ as a later entry to dummy. Win whatever is led next and play to A♦, ruff a diamond with a **high** trump in hand. Now, lead 7♠ to dummy's J♠ and ruff a fourth diamond **high** – establishing dummy's final diamond as a winner. Now, if trumps break 2-2, you can play 2♠ to dummy's 5♠ to enjoy the last diamond, on which you throw the club loser.

67 / PLANNING NO-TRUMP CONTRACTS – COUNT YOUR WINNERS

In a NT contract the best strategy is to count your tricks. If you have enough tricks to make your contract, play them out. If you do not have sufficient tricks for your contract, except in rare circumstances, it is not right to cash any winners until you have established the extra tricks. The reason is that your opponents will be delighted if you denude your hand of its stoppers (high cards) in each suit. The moment they gain the lead, they will have a field-day cashing unexpected winners in those suits.

NT contracts are a race between declarer and defenders as to who can establish their long suit first. The defence have a vital advantage of being on lead; declarer must play accurately to survive this attack.

This hand requires simple, but clear, thinking:

Dealer South	♠ A9		N	E	S	W
N/S Game	♥ K8		–	–	1H	NB
	♦ Q964		2C	NB	2NT	NB
	♣ Q10987		3NT			

♠ QJ1087		♠ 542
♥ 1062		♥ 9754
♦ 873		♦ A52
♣ A3		♣ A62

	♠ K63
	♥ AQJ3
	♦ KJ10
	♣ J54

Q♠ led: declarer counts his top tricks, and plans which suit to attack for his extra tricks.

He has two spade winners, four heart winners, and no other immediate tricks. Usually, it is correct to attack the suit in which you hold most cards between your two hands, to establish your extra tricks.

However, the declarer – Roland Saillard – lavished on this deal a little more thought and realised that this isn't always the case. Having won trick 1, declarer has only one spade stopper remaining and, should he attack clubs, he will lose the lead twice before any new tricks are set up. Clearly, he is doomed to lose the race – the opponents will cash their spade winners, and defeat the contract by one.

The declarer has six top tricks: he requires three more. Diamonds will provide those three tricks, losing the lead, crucially, only once. At trick 2, Roland attacked this suit until A♦ was dislodged, regained the lead by winning the spade continuation, and cashed his nine tricks before the opposition could regain control.

68 / KEEP FINESSES AS A LAST RESORT; TRY TO PLAN AN ELIMINATION ENDPLAY

When you first meet finesses, they seem quite a good deal offering a whole 50% chance of making a trick you might otherwise lose. As you improve, you should develop a healthy attitude of scorn for a mere 50%, and be looking for a better line; preferably one which offers a 100% chance.

If you must take a finesse, leave it until the last moment. By then, you may have gained more information about your opponents' hands. If it is a single finesse, you might know that it cannot possibly win, and play for an unlikely, but better, chance of the missing honour falling (see Tip 58). Facing a two-way finesse (one which can be taken through either opponent), delay until the end of the hand, providing maximum insight as to the missing card's likely position.

Better yet, avoid the finesse altogether. To endplay your opponents, to force them to take the finesse for you – wresting control from fate – is deeply satisfying.

This classic, simple example of an elimination endplay was my introduction to the play, and impressed me immediately:

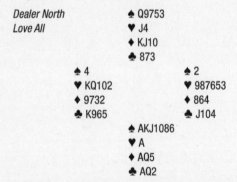

    Dealer North   ♠ Q9753
    Love All   ♥ J4
                          ♦ KJ10
                          ♣ 873

    ♠ 4   ♠ 2
    ♥ KQ102   ♥ 987653
    ♦ 9732   ♦ 864
    ♣ K965   ♣ J104

                          ♠ AKJ1086
                          ♥ A
                          ♦ AQ5
                          ♣ AQ2

West leads K♥ against South's 6S contract. With a certain low club loser, declarer faces the prospect of relying on a finesse with Q♣ for his contract. However, the finesse can be side-stepped. Winning the first trick, declarer draws trumps and plays out all his diamonds. Now, he leads J♥ from dummy, discarding 2♣ – his certain loser. West who, from the lead, is marked with Q♥, wins – and is endplayed. If he leads a red suit, declarer can ruff in dummy and discard Q♣ from his hand; if West plays a club, the lead comes around to South, taking the finesse for you.

The key was to ensure that there were trumps left in both hands (for the ruff and discard potential), and that diamonds are eliminated from both hands, thus denying West any safe suit with which to exit. Finally, an exit card was required to throw West on lead. J♥ was perfect for this, and playing 2♣ on it as a loser-on-loser play (see Tip 63) ensured that West was forced to win.

69 / MAKE THE HAND WITH THE MOST TRUMPS THE MASTER HAND – AUTOMATIC DUMMY REVERSAL

Usually declarer's hand either contains more trumps than dummy, or the same length but with more points. In these situations it is standard to trump your hand's losers in dummy, retaining the trump length in your own hand for drawing trumps.

When dummy holds more trumps than you, it is usually right to treat dummy as the master hand, and play the deal 'upside-down'. I describe this as an 'automatic dummy reversal': you ruff dummy's losers in your own hand. This situation is likely to occur after using Transfers, or with conventions such as 'Asptro'. Sometimes, even completely natural bidding, like 1H-4H, results in dummy holding more trumps than declarer.

A traditional Dummy Reversal goes one step further: declarer starts with more trumps than dummy, but they are used for ruffing, and dummy's trumps then become the controlling holding. This is a tough technique, but well worth studying.

In this example of an Automatic Dummy Reversal, if the declarer was North instead of South, the hand would be played normally. However, the declarer is indeed South:

Dealer North	♠ QJ1097	N	E	S	W
Love All	♥ A84	NB	NB	1NT	NB
	♦ 853	2H	NB	**2S**	
	♣ 32				

♠ A8	♠ 542
♥ 7652	♥ KQ109
♦ KQ107	♦ J6
♣ Q108	♣ K976

♠ K63
♥ J3
♦ A942
♣ AJ54

After a simple Transfer sequence, South plays in 2S and West leads K♦. Declarer notes that dummy contains more trumps than him, and plans to treat dummy as the master hand. In dummy, he has: one trump, two hearts, two diamonds, and one club to lose – that is one too many. However, a heart ruff in hand eliminates one loser, and so that is his plan. Winning A♦, he leads J♥, and runs it (merely as a duck) to East. A diamond comes back and E/W score two more tricks. When South regains the lead, he plays 3♥ to A♥ and ruffs 8♥ in his own hand. Now, he begins to draw trumps. Nothing horrifying befalls him and he emerges with his eight tricks.

There are other scenarios: if declarer starts to draw trumps before ruffing a heart in his own hand, he never comes to an eighth trick. Similarly, if West leads ♠A8, and East plays a third round later, declarer is a trick short as well.

70 / IN A 4-3 TRUMP FIT, TAKE CARE TO KEEP CONTROL

An eight-card fit is desirable because you hold the clear majority of trumps. From time to time, by design or otherwise, you will find yourself in the less comfortable position of playing a 4-3 trump fit. The danger here is that, unless the trumps break 3-3, which is only about a one-in-three chance, one of your opponents holds as many trumps as you. Ruff just once in your own hand, and you may lose control of the trumps altogether, and then it is only a matter of time before you go under. (I know this is unpleasant stuff, but it's better we face it together ...)

Unless your trumps are solid, with a 4-3 fit, it is almost always a good idea to duck the first round of play in the trump suit, so that your opponents win their trump trick whilst you still control the hand. It may also be important to keep trumps in dummy to prevent the opponents from forcing you to trump in your own hand.

This sometimes leads to some bizarre underleading of high cards but, providing you are happy with the principles involved, you might find these plays at the table.

Dealer West	♠ Q75	N	E	S	W
Game All	♥ A4	–	–	–	1H
	♦ KQJ4	Dbl	NB	4S	
	♣ A953				

	♠ J2		♠ 10984
	♥ KQJ1092		♥ 765
	♦ A7		♦ 10962
	♣ 1074		♣ 86

	♠ AK63
	♥ 83
	♦ 853
	♣ KQJ2

K♥ led. Declarer faces a heart and a diamond loser, plus the likelihood of a trump loser. But, if careless, the play might run: win trick 1, three rounds of trumps, switch to diamonds; West wins, plays two hearts, forcing South to ruff with his final trump. When East ruffs in with 10♠, E/W cash two more heart tricks, declarer now void in trumps.

To avoid this scenario, declarer has only to recognise that, as he almost certainly has to lose a trump trick, it is better he does so whilst still in control. He wins trick 1 with A♥, and plays a small trump from both hands. E/W cannot attack hearts effectively now, because dummy still contains trumps with which to ruff, leaving South with the trump length sufficient to keep control. Declarer dislodges A♦, and then draws the remaining trumps, emerging with 10 tricks.

The principle of leading your long suit to shorten the declarer's holding, and take him out of control, is demonstrated particularly well here, as shown by the result of the careless play scenario. It should remain a constant ambition of the defence to attack declarer's trump holding, virtually at all times.

71 / PUT YOURSELF IN THE MIND OF THE DEFENDER TO HELP YOU PLACE THE MISSING CARDS

Watching very good players can boost your own game immensely, playing with them even more so. So, when the high cards resolutely migrate to the hands either side of me, I leave my modest game at TGR club, and head to the 'Big Game' tables. Here, they do battle for vast stakes – always entertaining to kibitz. Laydown contracts immediately receive the treatment their name suggests and overtricks are not counted, so the number of hands played per hour is pretty high.

One occasion resulted in my being party to a valuable piece of advice from the great Zia Mahmood. The scene was a relaxed game which, at the time I rolled up, featured Zia in partnership with top-ranked American Bob Hamman, against the mad genius, Irving Rose, and Martin Barber. Zia had reached a tense 4H contract, in which he lost the lead whilst establishing his side-suit. At this point, Martin Barber led a small diamond, and Zia faced this position:

```
              ♦ KJ4
♦ 3 led                    ♦ ?
              ♦ 75
```

The lead was a good one, forcing Zia to decide the suit before he had had time to establish his side suit and discard his losers. If he mis-guessed the position of the honours, he would go down. To my surprise, Zia scarcely paused before rising with K♦, which held the trick. He then spread his hand, the contract secure.

'I thought it was quite a good lead,' Martin Barber joked.

'It wouldn't have been so bad,' I agreed, 'if he'd even stopped to think about it …'

Zia turned to me. 'I don't think in this position,' he told me. 'Think about it: would you have led from ♦Qxxx if dummy held ♦KJx?'

I thought about it for a moment, and agreed that I wouldn't, fearing that declarer might hold ♦A10x, and that I would solve the position for him. Zia jotted it down, and you can see that leading a diamond there is completely wrong.

```
              ♦ KJx
♦ Qxxx                     ♦?
              ♦ A10x
```

'But,' Zia continued, warming to his theme, 'you would happily lead from ♦Axx, because you know that it cannot cost a trick and, if partner holds Q♦, you may gain a tempo. You know that, so I know that. That's why I don't need to think …'

Of course, Zia has the benefit of having a mind that has worked all that out in advance, but his advice has saved me much angst since, because I know that whilst a good player would never make an opening lead away from an Ace except in peculiar circumstances, he will happily lead away from it when he can see the King, or KJx, to his left. Equally, he will lead from Qxx as an opening lead, but will be most reluctant to do so if he can see KJx in dummy.

72 / FINESSES (1): NEVER LEAD AN HONOUR WITHOUT THE CARD BENEATH IT

This is another easy tip, but too many social players squander their contracts this way. I had to include it. How would you try to make two tricks from this suit?

♥ A42
•
♥ Q53

Your best chance for two tricks would be to lead low towards Q♥, hoping that RHO held K♥. If he does, he must decide whether to play it before you decide whether to play your Queen. If K♥ is sitting over Q♥, you must lose the trick.

Was that obvious? Or might you have been tempted to lead Q♥? If you do that, you will never make a trick with Q♥, because if LHO holds K♥, he will always cover Q♥, forcing you to play A♥, leaving you with no winning cards in the suit; if RHO holds K♥, he will beat Q♥.

Never lead a high card for a finesse without at least one of the cards immediately below it. Leading Q♥ for the finesse in this next example would be correct:

♥ A42
•
♥ QJ10

Now, if LHO covers what you lead, you win, and you hold the next highest cards also.

Very rarely, you will encounter a situation where it is correct to lead a high card without the card immediately beneath it. However, as you will see, you must instead hold several other significant high cards for the play to be successful:

```
                ♥ Qxx
♥ xx                        ♥ KJx
                ♥ A109xx
```

Here, RHO opens the bidding, but you play the hand. It would be correct to lead Q♥ from dummy, playing through RHO. As he bid, you place him with K♥ or J♥ – possibly both – and this play picks up the suit for one loser. RHO will cover Q♥ with K♥; you will win with A♥ and still have ♥109 to cope with his J♥. If LHO actually holds K♥, you lose Q♥ to him, but later finesse for J♥ through RHO, with your ♥A109 as the tenace.

If you felt that LHO was more likely to hold the high cards, you would lead 10♥, planning to finesse first for J♥, and later for K♥ if necessary.

None of these plays would be correct without 9♥ in your hand. Without it, you merely ensure tricks for the opposition.

73 / FINESSES (2): WHAT TO DO WHEN YOU KNOW WHERE A CARD LIES

Sometimes you will know where a key card lies. This knowledge will often be gleaned through your counting skills (see Tips 51 and 52). However, if your usually inept opponents seem to have second sight, it may be that, like me, you are not holding your cards up ... Even when you do know the position of a card, it may not always be good news:

```
            ♥ A52
♥ Q74              ♥ 10986
            ♥ KJ3
```

You know your LHO holds Q♥, but you cannot pick it up with a finesse. Instead, you must now seek to endplay LHO, forcing him to lead a heart to you.

At other times, you can invent a chance for yourself:

```
            ♥ A52
♥ Q74              ♥ 10863
            ♥ KJ9
```

With no endplay chances, and knowing that Q♥ lies with LHO, your extra chance lies with RHO holding 10♥. Lead J♥, expecting LHO to cover it with Q♥, and win with A♥. Now, lead 2♥ and, when RHO plays small, finesse with 9♥. If LHO holds both Q♥ and 10♥, I think you were doomed.

A good player showed me this play many years ago, but while it will fool some, it rarely succeeds against good players.

Dealer North	♠ 987	**N**	**E**	**S**	**W**
E/W Game	♥ 84	NB	1NT	Dbl	2C
	♦ AJ10986	2D	NB	**3NT**	
	♣ 32				

```
        ♠ 987
        ♥ 84
        ♦ AJ10986
        ♣ 32
♠ 1032          ♠ KQ5
♥ 7652          ♥ KQ109
♦ 74            ♦ Q53
♣ QJ108         ♣ 976
        ♠ AJ64
        ♥ AJ3
        ♦ K2
        ♣ AK54
```

Playing social Rubber bridge with Jack Marks, we reached the delicate contract of 3NT after West had bid 2C as an escape from 1NT doubled and my partner had shown his diamond suit. On Q♣ lead by West – presumably promising J♣ – I knew that East must hold all the remaining high cards. As diamonds could be my only salvation, I had to decide whether it was possible that East held just ♦Qx. Reasoning that West might hold a five-card club suit for her bid, I decided that East was likely to be long elsewhere, and that Q♦ doubleton was unlikely. All normal finesses in diamonds were impossible, as there was no other entry to dummy, but there was one obscure play that just might work.

Winning the lead with K (see Tip 60), I led 2♦ at trick 2, putting in J♦ from dummy. East pounced on this with Q♦ and returned a club. I could now win, and then play K♦, overtaking it with A♦ in dummy, and run down the diamonds.

74 / ON LEAD (1): LEAD TOP OF A SEQUENCE RATHER THAN FOURTH HIGHEST

When most people are asked what they lead against a no-trump contract, they reply, 'fourth highest'. It is peculiar that the second most important lead is remembered so vividly, whilst the more attacking, yet safer, lead is often forgotten.

Once you have decided which suit to play, you should always play the top card from a sequence of honours.

A top of sequence lead attacks by pushing out declarer's high cards, but does not risk leading away from an honour. It is the ideal lead.

If you are on lead against a suit contract, then merely two cards in sequence will suffice: against a NT contract, you require three significant cards. If you do not hold a sufficient sequence, then you lead fourth highest card. Sequences should be led from AKQ, down to 1097, but any lower sequence is irrelevant, and should be treated as non-touching small cards, and the lead made as described in the next tip.

Three cards in a row (KQJ) is a sequence; two cards, and the next but one, (KQ10) is a broken sequence; a sequence or broken sequence with one high card above it (Q1098 or KJ108) is known as an internal, or interior, sequence.

In each case, you would lead the top card in the sequence.

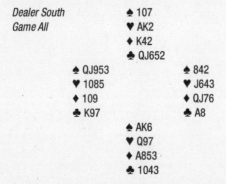

Dealer South
Game All

	♠ 107	
	♥ AK2	
	♦ K42	
	♣ QJ652	
♠ QJ953		♠ 842
♥ 1085		♥ J643
♦ 109		♦ QJ76
♣ K97		♣ A8
	♠ AK6	
	♥ Q97	
	♦ A853	
	♣ 1043	

A careless choice of opening lead cost E/W a vulnerable Game contract, in a teams of four match. In the first room, against South's 3NT contract, West led Q♠, which South ducked. West continued with J♠. South won, set about dislodging ♣AK, and eventually lost two club tricks, and three spade tricks, for one off.

In the other room, West led his fourth highest spade: the five. Dummy hopped up with 10♠ and this held the trick. Now, declarer had time to establish his clubs, and brought home his contract.

The hand demonstrates the reason to lead top card of a broken sequence; if dummy or declarer holds the missing honour (here, 10♠) singleton or doubleton, its value is annulled. If partner holds it, he discards it (see Tip 77) to indicate that it is safe for you to continue leading the suit.

75 / ON LEAD (2): DON'T LEAD FOURTH HIGHEST WITHOUT AN HONOUR

When leading, a low card led denotes interest in the suit. For a fourth highest lead, your suit must be headed by an honour card. Many players count the 10 as an honour when defending. However, unless the 10 has 'friends' – in a sequence – it should not be counted as an honour.

When your suit is not headed by an honour, lead the highest or second highest of the suit, allowing partner to distinguish between a top-of-rubbish high card lead and an encouraging low card.

These understandings allow you to find the correct line of defence on hands like this one:

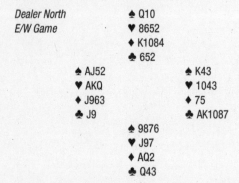

Against West's 3NT contract, my friend Suzanne Saillard led 8♥, indicating no honour in her suit. Immediately, I could place ♥AKQ with West, accounting for over half his advertised points. At trick 2, declarer led J♣, and I won with Q♣.

What are my options? Declarer has three hearts and four club tricks. If he holds A♠, he also has two spade tricks, giving him his contract. So, knowing that a heart return is wrong, it's relatively easy to find the switch to A♦ and then Q♦. Partner takes the third and fourth diamond tricks and the contract is down.

If you do not recognise that 8♥ denied an honour, you are likely to return a heart and declarer scores his 3NT with ease.

76 / ON LEAD (3): AGAINST NO-TRUMP CONTRACTS, IF YOU ARE VERY WEAK, DON'T LEAD YOUR OWN LONG SUIT

The opening lead against a no-trump contract is the one time the opposition have the advantage over the declarer; they can begin to establish their long suit immediately. Often, when the right lead is made, a NT contract fails; if the lead is wrong, the contract makes. But what is the right lead? A long suit from a hand with sufficient entries – or communication with partner's hand – to lead it repeatedly until established, and then cash winning tricks.

♠ J9742
♥ 85
♦ 432
♣ 865

What would you lead from this hand, after bidding of 1NT-3NT?

4♠? Well, it *might* be the right lead.

Think back to the definition of the right lead: you require entries to continue playing the suit and then to cash your winners. Even if a spade strikes gold, you'll never regain the lead to enjoy your established tricks.

When you hold a hand which is obviously weaker than your partner's, remember that this is a partnership game: start working out what your partner might play, if it were he on lead.

You're guessing, of course, but you still stand a better chance of finding the winning lead than blithely letting a spade darken the green baize.

As the opposition have failed to use Stayman, dummy may well hold no four-card major suit, so your partner could hold five hearts. Try 8♥. If he can win, return the suit, and regain the lead – you may just become the hero.

You have to be prepared to face the occasional disaster when you lead like this, as I did in the example below. If you are playing with an intelligent partner, he will realise that you have made a good shot at finding a sensible lead and, this time, it has failed.

Dealer South
Love All

N	***E***	***S***	***W***
–	–	1NT	NB
3NT			

North:
♠ A7
♥ 84
♦ 2
♣ KQJ106543

West	East
♠ Q432	♠ 10985
♥ 532	♥ KJ106
♦ 643	♦ AKQJ7
♣ 972	♣ –

South:
♠ KJ6
♥ AQ97
♦ 10983
♣ A8

My regular partner, who has a global reputation for eye-rolling at the bridge table, could only laugh when I found this awe-inspiring lead against 3NT in a Rubber bridge match:

Convinced that 2♠ was not right, I considered a heart, before plumping for 9♣. Dummy was not quite what I was hoping for … We were hysterical, but the opposition, who were taking the whole tacky affair far too seriously, reeled off each trick with barely disguised glee.

'A diamond would have defeated me,' the declarer pronounced po-faced at the end, when that was abundantly clear anyway.

Now, I'm not a violent man, but …

77 / JETTISON HIGH CARDS TO SHOW YOUR PARTNER HIS SEQUENCE IS COMPLETE

You are in 3NT, and your opponent leads K♥. You hold ♥642 in dummy, opposite ♥AJ7 in your hand. What do you play at trick 1?

It's correct to duck, forming the 'Bath Coup'. This play prevents the leader from playing another heart without giving you two tricks; the suit is, effectively, frozen.

Now, put yourself in the defender's shoes. You lead K♥ from ♥KQ10xx, dummy goes down with three little cards, partner plays small, and declarer ducks. What do you lead at trick 2?

You know that partner does not hold A♥, as he would have played it (see below), so declarer has it. What about J♥? From the initial example, you can see that it is quite possible that declarer holds J♥ and A♥. So, how do you know whether to continue leading hearts, or to switch?

The key lies in your partner's card. Because the lead of an honour must be part of a sequence, the general rule is this: when your partner leads an honour card against a NT contract, if you hold an honour, you must play it immediately. Since partner has played a low card, he cannot hold either A♥ or J♥.

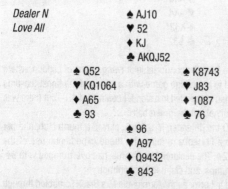

Dealer N	♠ AJ10
Love All	♥ 52
	♦ KJ
	♣ AKQJ52

♠ Q52		♠ K8743
♥ KQ1064		♥ J83
♦ A65		♦ 1087
♣ 93		♣ 76

	♠ 96
	♥ A97
	♦ Q9432
	♣ 843

This principle ensured that defeating this contract is simple. Against 3NT, West leads K♥, East drops J♥, and West continues to lead hearts until A♥ appears. When he wins A♦, he can cash the remaining heart winners. Simple and stress free.

I read once that the average length of a serious bridge partnership is only two years, eight months. This type of considerate partnership play should, at a stroke, improve those figures, reduce the divorce rate, and cut down on expensive household breakages.

78 / RUFF HIGH TO PROMOTE YOUR PARTNER'S TRUMPS

The principle of ruffing with a high trump to promote a trump trick for partner is important, especially when partner leads a suit which declarer is known to be able to ruff. No intelligent partner would subject you to an over-ruff for no purpose so, in this situation, you should make a point of ruffing in high.

When a famous whisky maker was the major sponsor of bridge in the UK, this story formed part of their folklore. It was my invention, the characters loosely based on real people: you know who you are!

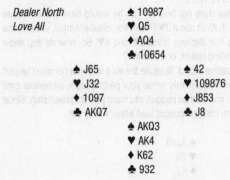

Dealer North
Love All

```
                    ♠ 10987
                    ♥ Q5
                    ♦ AQ4
                    ♣ 10654
♠ J65                               ♠ 42
♥ J32                               ♥ 109876
♦ 1097                              ♦ J853
♣ AKQ7                              ♣ J8
                    ♠ AKQ3
                    ♥ AK4
                    ♦ K62
                    ♣ 932
```

There comes to us a tale from the comfortable drawing rooms of London, where Mrs McDougal returned to her bridge game with a trolley of the finest tea-time delicacies. Her partner had succeeded in a slender contract of 4S – but there was not all joy and equanimity about the green baize ...

Having led out ♣AKQ the defender, Mrs Black, played a fourth club, and her French partner, Madame Porteous, a lady who made expeditious use of the tunnel, had ruffed with 2♠. The declarer, Mrs Filigree, had overtrumped with 3♠, drawn the remaining trumps, and claimed her contract.

The hostess watched in horror as the formidable Mrs Black scrabbled through the overturned cards to retrieve her partner's 4♠ which she tapped with a raised eyebrow and a slender, brittle nail.

'If you had ruffed with 4♠, Madame,' she preached, 'declarer would have been forced to part with her Q♠, and my Jack becomes a winner! My mother always told me never to send a boy to do a man's job!'

'But they were both boys,' came the Gallic protestation.

Mrs Black drew herself up to her full width: 'Then you should have sent the older one!'

122

Mrs McDougal looked from one flushed face to another in the silence. Suddenly, a means dawned on her to retrieve her genteel afternoon from social infamy. She nudged away her trolley of dainties, and poured each guest a glass of her favourite whisky from a bottle retrieved from a hidden drawer.

'Look at you now,' she scolded, taking a man-sized draft of the elixir, 'arguing over a bridge hand … We've missed tea again …'

79 / PLAY THE CARD YOU ARE KNOWN TO HOLD

One area which distinguishes true experts from average players is the concealment of information from the opposition. As declarer, most energy is spent trying to form a coherent plan to fulfil our contract. In defence, however, it is beneficial to form a smoke-screen to disguise the contents of your hand. To achieve this, do not produce cards which your opponents don't know about; instead play those you are known to hold already:

```
                    ♥ AQ642
        ♥ KJ10                  ♥ 987
                    ♥ 53
```

The declarer, South, leads 3♥, you – to the left – play 10♥, and he finesses with Q♥. When this wins, declarer knows you hold K♥. He now plays A♥, and you play J♥ – that is a card he did not know you held. You have provided extra information. Instead, when A♥ is cashed, since K♥ and J♥ are now equal, drop the King. This may cause declarer to place your partner with four hearts, and abandon a winning line.

The beauty of these plays is that, whilst all good players know that you might be false-carding, they cannot be certain. Keeping a good player guessing is your best chance of beating him.

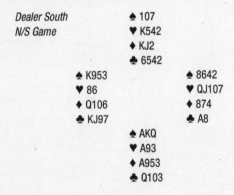

```
Dealer South          ♠ 107
N/S Game              ♥ K542
                      ♦ KJ2
                      ♣ 6542
        ♠ K953                  ♠ 8642
        ♥ 86                    ♥ QJ107
        ♦ Q106                  ♦ 874
        ♣ KJ97                  ♣ A8
                      ♠ AKQ
                      ♥ A93
                      ♦ A953
                      ♣ Q103
```

This hand demonstrates the principle perfectly:

Against South's 3NT, West led 7♣ and E/W took the first four club tricks. When declarer played on diamonds, he led 3♦ and finessed with J♦. He then cashed K♦, on which West nonchalantly dropped Q♦. The expert declarer, underestimating one of my students, assumed that East held four diamonds to the 10, and he led 2♦ and, when East followed low, he finessed with 9♦ and lost to West's 10♦.

Notice that, if West had blithely played 10♦ on the second round, declarer would have had no losing option and fulfils his contract with ease.

80 / UNBLOCK THE FLOW OF A SUIT BY PLAYING THE HIGH CARD FROM THE SHORTER HOLDING

This tip is vital for both declarer and defenders. The difference being, of course, that the declarer can see both his own hand and dummy – although sometimes I wonder – whilst defenders play with only partial knowledge.

How would you play these suits, if you had no other entry back to the bottom hand?

a) ♦A3 **b)** ♦K8

♦KQJ104 ♦AQJ94

a) Play low to the Ace, and 3♦ back to your winners. If you don't play the Ace first, you end up in the top hand, unable to cash your remaining winners.
b) Play 4♦ the King (playing the high card from the shorter holding) and 8♦ back to hand.

This is easy to see as declarer, but you must also do it when defending:

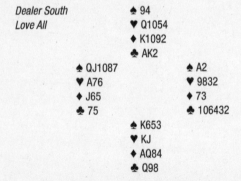

```
Dealer South        ♠ 94
Love All            ♥ Q1054
                    ♦ K1092
                    ♣ AK2
  ♠ QJ1087                        ♠ A2
  ♥ A76                           ♥ 9832
  ♦ J65                           ♦ 73
  ♣ 75                            ♣ 106432
                    ♠ K653
                    ♥ KJ
                    ♦ AQ84
                    ♣ Q98
```

West leads Q♠ against South's 3NT. Following Tip 77, East already wants to overtake with A♠, but it is essential here to prevent the suit from blocking. If you play 2♠ and West leads a second spade, you win with the Ace and cannot lead again. When your partner leads an honour, if your length in the suit is likely to be shorter than his, you should overtake his honour with your high card, and return the suit to him.

To avoid this, remember to play the high card from the shorter holding. West must hold ♠QJ10 so it is quite safe to overtake and return the suit. West continues until South's K♠ is dislodged, and when he takes A♥, the remaining spades can be cashed to defeat 3NT.

81 / DON'T WIN A FINESSE IMMEDIATELY IF THE DECLARER MUST TAKE IT A SECOND TIME

This principle is similar to the logic involved in playing the card you are known to hold; this time, you *withhold* information from declarer, hoping that he misplaces the cards.

You need to be certain that declarer *will* take the finesse again, and that by ducking, you do not give him the trick he needs to fulfil his contract. And you have to be ready for the play: to pause will give away the swindle. If in doubt, use this tip against NT contracts only when declarer is obviously establishing his long suit to make extra tricks.

This technique worked a treat in my first international competition, a European 'Friendly Games', in which bridge was the leading mind-sport. Renowned teacher Elizabeth Hallifax and her partner played with Quentin Moore and me, fresh from winning the National Schools Championship. The hugely enjoyable event concentrated as much on fine Dutch hospitality as it did on the sports themselves. Elizabeth protected us from the worst excesses of alcohol (unselfishly consuming it herself), and we were required to put in a decent performance at the bridge table.

Q's anticipation and casual duck led to a Game swing on this hand:

Dealer N	♠ AQ		N	E	S	W
Love All	♥ 87		1D	NB	1S	NB
	♦ AQJ109		2C	NB	**3NT**	
	♣ 7432					

♠ K76	♠ J1092
♥ A9632	♥ 1054
♦ 5	♣ K872
♣ K1098	♣ Q6

	♠ 8543
	♥ KQJ
	♦ 643
	♣ AJ5

I led 3♥, partner played 10♥, and the French declarer won Q♥. She now took a diamond finesse, which Q allowed to hold. Since the diamonds are her only hope, she returned to hand with A♣, Q dropping Q♣. She repeated the diamond finesse – and I played 2♥ – suggesting I liked clubs. Quentin won with K♦ and switched

128

to 6♣. Declarer's ♣J5 were now beaten, and I was able to cash three club tricks, plus A♥ to defeat the contract.

Had Q won the first trick with K♦, declarer can win his return, finesse with Q♠, and make her 3NT. That is what happened at the other table.

82 / SHOW COUNT IF DECLARER IS PLAYING TO A LONG SUIT IN AN ENTRYLESS DUMMY

When to take your Ace can be a really tough defensive decision. However, if your partner helps you, it can become easy. Here's a classic example:

				N	E	S	W
Dealer South		♠ 973		*N*	*E*	*S*	*W*
E/W Game		♥ 85		–	–	2NT	NB
		♦ KQJ109		3NT			
		♣ 643					

```
              ♠ QJ1085              ♠ 62
              ♥ Q76                 ♥ KJ104
              ♦ 652                 ♦ A74
              ♣ 87                  ♣ 10952

                      ♠ AK4
                      ♥ A932
                      ♦ 83
                      ♣ AKQJ
```

West leads Q♠, and declarer wins, and leads 3♦ towards dummy. East and West play low, and declarer leads another diamond. Frightened of establishing the suit while South may still hold another diamond, East ducks a second time. This play might have been right but, with two diamond tricks, South now has nine tricks.

How could East have known that it was safe – and vital – to take the second round of diamonds with his A♦?

Whenever there is a long suit in an entryless dummy, both defenders should signal their count (or length) in the suit. With an even number of cards, play a high card first; with an odd number of cards, play your lowest card first. Whoever faces the decision of when to play the Ace can now count the suit, and deduce the distribution around the table.*

Here, when South first leads a diamond, West plays 2♦, East 4♦. When declarer plays a second diamond, East counts: three diamonds in partner's hand (an odd number is nearly always three cards), five in dummy, three in his hand – leaving declarer with only two. Now he knows to win the trick, reassured that declarer will have no more. This holds declarer to only one diamond trick, and leaves him short for his contract.

When dummy does hold outside entries, or when the declarer is reeling off winners from a solid suit, your signals may have a different meaning – see Tip 83.

A low card from partner – showing an odd number – is very often indicating three cards. A high card – indicating an even number – is nearly always showing two or four cards. Using this information, plus what you see in dummy, and from what you have learned from the auction, you should be able to place the correct number of cards in the two hidden hands. It takes some effort but, once you are used to it, the information it affords you can be priceless.

Some partnerships play that a high card shows an odd number of cards; a low card shows an even number of cards – so-called 'reverse count'.

83 / MAKE A SUIT-PREFERENCE SIGNAL WHENEVER THE COUNT IS IRRELEVANT

This tip is for more experienced players and partnerships; many social bridge Games operate quite happily when the only signals shown are for more cucumber sandwiches.

In the previous tip, you saw that it is often advantageous to indicate the length you hold in suits. However, when such a signal cannot be of interest, good players substitute it with a Suit-Preference signal to indicate which of the other suits they would like led. This is a direct cousin of the Suit-Preference discard, which we'll look at next.

If you are involved in trying to win the trick, then obviously you cannot also be signalling. However, if you are merely following suit:

- playing the lowest card in the suit led, by your opponent, suggests interest in a low-ranking suit;
- playing the highest cards in the suit led indicates interest in a high-ranking suit.

Dutch pair Berry Westra and Enri Leufkens demonstrated their confidence in the *Sunday Times*/The Macallan International Pairs. Their opponents were the best British pair for decades – Andrew Robson and Tony Forrester:

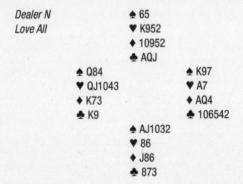

```
Dealer N              ♠ 65
Love All              ♥ K952
                      ♦ 10952
                      ♣ AQJ
          ♠ Q84                  ♠ K97
          ♥ QJ1043               ♥ A7
          ♦ K73                  ♦ AQ4
          ♣ K9                   ♣ 106542
                      ♠ AJ1032
                      ♥ 86
                      ♦ J86
                      ♣ 873
```

Like the rest of the field, Andy Robson (East) found himself playing in 3NT, with South leading J♠. Robson won in hand with K♠, and cashed A♥ and another, North playing 2♥ and 5♥. Robson persevered with hearts, but North refused again, dropping 9♥. Finally, he won K♥, and then played to his partner's A♠.

At this point, South knows that the defence must defeat the contract immediately. North's play of his lowest hearts at all times clearly indicated that he wanted a club led. When South did this, N/S took three club tricks to beat the contract – a defence not found at other tables.

84 / WHEN DISCARDING, THROW AWAY THE SUIT YOU ARE LEAST INTERESTED IN YOUR PARTNER LEADING

Traditionally, Rubber bridge players tend to discard high cards in suits they want, and low ones in suits they dislike. Against NTs, where the length of the suit is its strength, this can prove a very costly method.

It is much more logical, not to mention economical, to make your first discard from the suit you least want your partner to lead. In other words, you are throwing away what you don't want.

That simple system in itself is an improvement over the old-fashioned methods, and can be adopted for defence against NTs or suit contracts.

In addition, many players include Suit Preference, or Mckenney, signals within the discard. From the size of the card you throw away from your least favourite suit, you indicate which other suit you would like. When you discard, you are clearly not interested in the suit you cannot follow to, nor in the suit you have played – the suit you least want. There are, therefore, only two suits you can be interested in:

- if you want the higher-ranking of the remaining two suits, discard a high card in the suit you least want;
- if you want the lower-ranking, discard the lowest card in the suit you least want.

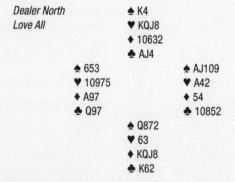

Dealer North
Love All

```
                    ♠ K4
                    ♥ KQJ8
                    ♦ 10632
                    ♣ AJ4
        ♠ 653                   ♠ AJ109
        ♥ 10975                 ♥ A42
        ♦ A97                   ♦ 54
        ♣ Q97                   ♣ 10852
                    ♠ Q872
                    ♥ 63
                    ♦ KQJ8
                    ♣ K62
```

These discards are simple and powerful; your partnership confidence will be boosted considerably.

Taken from a high-stake Rubber bridge game, here is a suit-preference discard in action:

Against South's 3NT, West led 10♥, and dummy was allowed to win with K♥. Declarer played three rounds of diamonds, West refusing until the third round – on which East threw 10♣, indicating interest in the higher-ranking suit: spades. West switched to 6♠ and East took dummy's K♠ and continued spades until South parted with Q♠. When East regained the lead with A♥, he could cash a further spade trick to defeat the contract.

Notice that East could not afford to discard a high spade to encourage West to lead that suit – it would have given the declarer the contract.

85 / DON'T COVER AN HONOUR WITH AN HONOUR IF YOU CAN'T PROMOTE A TRICK FOR YOUR SIDE

You cover an honour led by an opponent with your honour in an attempt to promote lower cards into winners for your side.

```
                    ♥ A75
      ♥ K96          •          ♥ 1042
                    ♥ QJ83
```

South leads Q♥; West covers with K♥. A♥ must be played and East's 10♥ is promoted to win the third round. If West fails to cover either Q♥ or J♥, East never scores his 10♥.

If there is any chance of promoting a trick for your side, cover an opponent's honour with an honour. However, when there is no chance of promotion for your side, you must take care *not* to cover. Pause to consider your options. In the example above, it makes no difference if West thinks before playing his K♥ or low. South's plan is to finesse; knowing that West has K♥ is not much of an advantage.

In the following example, East must decide whether to cover dummy's honour with his honour. The success or failure of the contract rests on his decision:

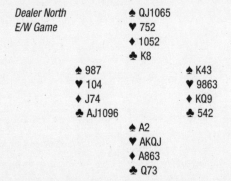

```
Dealer North        ♠ QJ1065
E/W Game            ♥ 752
                    ♦ 1052
                    ♣ K8
      ♠ 987                      ♠ K43
      ♥ 104                      ♥ 9863
      ♦ J74                      ♦ KQ9
      ♣ AJ1096                   ♣ 542
                    ♠ A2
                    ♥ AKQJ
                    ♦ A863
                    ♣ Q73
```

Against 3NT by South, West leads J♣ (see Tip 74), and dummy plays K♣, which wins. Q♠ is led: should East cover? If he does, South wins A♠, and runs five spades, four hearts and a diamond which, added to the club trick already made, makes 11 tricks.

The question East must ask himself is this: 'Is there any possibility that by covering I can promote a spade trick for our side?'

Definitely not. If South holds three spades, then it is vital that East does not part with his K♠ at all, even if it means losing it to A♠ eventually, since South is then cut off from dummy. If South has ♠Ax, then West holds three and with ♠QJ10 in dummy, none of his cards can possibly be promoted.

So, East should work out that it can never be right to cover Q♠ with K♠ here. Whatever South does now, he cannot score more than two spade tricks, four heart tricks, a club and a diamond, and that is not enough.

86 / ALWAYS LEAD A TRUMP AFTER OPPONENTS HAVE SHOWN SIMPLE PREFERENCE

A trump lead is not for when you can't think of anything better. Leading trumps often combines safety with attack – the perfect combination. The times when a trump lead stands out are when the opponents are short of points and rely on making extra tricks by trumping or cross-ruffing. Auctions such as 1H-4H, or 1S-2S-3S-4S, or after a simple preference sequence, all suggest a trump lead.

Do not lead a singleton trump; it often exposes partner's good holding to an immediate finesse. You can underlead the trump Ace, and often this is the most effective way.

Dealer North
Love All

♠ J103
♥ 5
♦ K8542
♣ KJ76

N	E	S	W
NB	NB	1S	NB
2D	NB	2H	NB
2S			

♠ A62　　　　　　　　♠ 54
♥ Q1076　　　　　　 ♥ A984
♦ QJ10　　　　　　　♦ A97
♣ 1098　　　　　　　♣ Q542

♠ KQ987
♥ KJ32
♦ 63
♣ A3

I played this hand during a strange match, held in Fiji:

After the simple preference sequence, I led 2♠. Declarer put in dummy's 10♠, which won. He led 5♥ from dummy, which East correctly ducked smoothly – see Tip 87 – and declarer played J♥, losing to my Q♥. Now, I cashed A♠ and another, exhausting dummy's supply. With no trumps to ruff his losing hearts, and both minor suit finesses failing, declarer ended up two tricks short. A more standard original lead of the unbid suit, 10♣, gives South time to ruff at least one heart, and possibly establish dummy's fourth club. As it was, the defence gave him no opportunity.

87 / WHEN A SINGLETON IS LED FROM DUMMY, PLAY SMALL EVEN IF YOU HOLD THE ACE

This tip may sound frightening but, generally, the second hand to play, plays low. What if you duck your Ace and later it gets trumped? The chances are, you still won't have forfeited a trick. Ducking in second position – for its deceptive element alone – will gain you hundreds of points in the long run. In these examples, South is playing with spades as trumps and he is attacking his side-suit:

In (a) 5♦ is led from dummy, and East plays 3♦ smoothly. Which card will declarer play? Almost certainly not K♦, for he should reason that if RHO held A♦, he would play it. So, declarer tries J♦, and partner wins Q♦. Even if South does play K♦, he still has three more diamonds to ruff, whereas, if you leap in with A♦, he requires only two ruffs. You'll make your Ace at the end.

In (b) 8♦ led, and East ducks. This time, declarer *will* win with K♦ or Q♦ (but he may try 10♦). However, again, he now has to ruff three diamonds in dummy, whereas if you smack down A♦ immediately, he only has to make one ruff.

The number of times you will lose by ducking is minute compared to the vast number of occasions on which it gains. Be prepared to play smoothly to maximise the effect. If you hesitate unduly when declarer leads dummy's singleton, you may give away that you hold the Ace.

Amongst experts, this play is so standard that as declarer you have no idea whether RHO holds the Ace when he plays small in such a situation. Against average players, when you are declarer, if your RHO plays low, assume that he does *not* hold the Ace, as most players leap in without even a thought.

The one occasion you should probably rise with your Ace is when you have a short holding, such as Ax or Axx, which the declarer might be able to ruff out easily. Also, if you require one trick to break the contract, you should usually make it and take no risk.

Against NT contracts, unless you have an urgent reason to gain the lead, never hurry to win tricks in the suit your opponent is attempting to establish.

88 / THINK ABOUT THE BIDDING AND DECLARER'S LIKELY PLAN BEFORE CHOOSING YOUR LEAD

Recalling the auction is important for defenders and declarer (see Tips 51 and 52). From it, try to map out a picture of the two opposing hands.

Against NTs, you usually lead your longest suit. However, when you have a choice of leads, draw inferences from the bidding to help you.

Did responder use Stayman? If not, he probably does not hold a four-card major. Could he have shown a major suit at the 1-level? If he could, but didn't, then he probably doesn't have one.

After a confident auction by opponents, attack with your lead as they hold good values and will make their contract unless you can score a ruff, or force them in trumps. In this situation, lead a singleton, or from a long, strong suit.

If the opposition seem uncertain of the correct contract, take no risk with your lead: try a trump, or top of a sequence of honours.

My partner, Peter Hardyment, used the auction to find the King lead from this uninspiring collection in the quarter-finals of the Devonshire Cup.

West	N	E	S	W
♠ QJ10	–	–	1C	NB
♥ J542	3C	3D	3S	NB
♦ 82	4S	NB	4NT	NB
♣ K962	5D	NB	5S	

At one table, West led 8♦ – his partner's suit. Declarer had no diamond losers and he could pick up the clubs without loss also, so the defence made only two tricks. My partner thought differently: South holds five clubs and four spades; North has four clubs also, so partner must be void. Sure enough, I ruffed at trick 1, and the contract failed.

Two Key Lead Ideas:

Since there are only two main means of getting rid of losers in suit contracts (see Tip 65), use the information gained from the bidding to help you determine the best line of attack:

- If there is likely to be a shortage in dummy which declarer can use to make ruffs, lead trumps to cut down that ruffing potential.
- If there could be a long, strong suit in dummy on which the declarer can throw his losers from hand, aggressively attack the other suits, even leading from honours.

89 / DROP YOUR QUEEN UNDER PARTNER'S ACE TO GUARANTEE THAT YOU CAN WIN THE NEXT TRICK

This is an important little play defence to suit contracts, particularly when you are short of entries.

When your partner leads an Ace from AK (or King if that is your style), you encourage or discourage him to continue leading the suit – by using 'attitude' signals (high card for encouragement; low card for discouragement). Traditionally, you only encourage if you have a doubleton or Qxx(x). The one time you do not play a high card with a doubleton is when you hold Queen doubleton; the drop of the Queen has a more important meaning: I can win the next round, if you want me on lead, play small now – either I hold the Jack, or I'm now void and can ruff.

Dealer East	♠ Q3		N	E	S	W
N/S Game	♥ 65		–	NB	1S	2C
	♦ AKQJ852		2D	NB	2S	NB
	♣ 76		4D	NB	4S	

	♠ 62			♠ 754	
	♥ AQ10			♥ 98743	
	♦ 96			♦ 107	
	♣ AK9842			♣ QJ5	

	♠ AKJ1098
	♥ KJ2
	♦ 43
	♣ 103

At one of their intensive bridge weekends, I tortured some favourite students with this deal. N/S play in 4S on the auction shown, and West leads A♣. The defenders at one table let the contract make but, at the other, Georgina and Mark Pumfrey showed how it should be done. At trick 1, seeing dummy's ultra-threatening diamond suit, George dropped Q♣ on her husband's A♣ lead; this caused Mark to put down his beer and think. Remembering its significance, he led 9♣ to George's Jack, and she switched smartly to a heart. The defence had four tricks before declarer knew what had hit him.

90 / MAKE DECLARER TRUMP IN HIS OWN HAND

Every declarer knows the frustration of a defender with lots of trumps. It might prevent them being drawn, or threaten a sudden ruff while you try to establish a side-suit. Yet, when defending, the same players seem reluctant to produce this situation by force – by making declarer trump in his own hand so that his trump holding is reduced.

It is always safe to make the declarer trump in his own hand, unless he is playing a dummy reversal – see Tip 69. An added advantage is that this makes declarer play side-suits himself – the best chance for the defence to take maximum tricks. Unless dummy contains a long suit, passive defence is the order of the day.

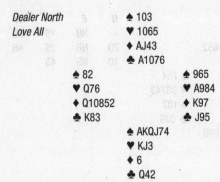

```
Dealer North          ♠ 103
Love All              ♥ 1065
                      ♦ AJ43
                      ♣ A1076
        ♠ 82                        ♠ 965
        ♥ Q76                       ♥ A984
        ♦ Q10852                    ♦ K97
        ♣ K83                       ♣ J95
                      ♠ AKQJ74
                      ♥ KJ3
                      ♦ 6
                      ♣ Q42
```

On this deal, East-West's steady defence provided their best hope of defeating declarer. Against South's 4S, West led 5♦ and declarer played A♦ from dummy. Attacking clubs, South led 6♣, losing Q♣ to West's K♣. West led 10♦ and this ran to South's ruff. Trumps were drawn and 10♣ finessed, losing to J♣. Again, East makes declarer trump in his own hand – by leading K♦. South ruffs and plays out clubs, pitching a low heart on the final one. Now, he led 5♥ and when East played small, he put in J♥. This lost to Q♥, and East made A♥ to defeat the contract. Declarer could have done much better, but E/W gave him no help and the mis-guess led to defeat. Uninspiring, unsexy, unglamorous – but solid defence.

When you or your partner hold four trumps or more, forcing declarer to ruff in hand can be a very destructive defence: the moment a defender holds more trumps than declarer, he takes over control of the hand.

When you hold four trumps, you often have a shortage elsewhere. Resist the temptation to lead your shortage. Go for the force, rather than ruffs in your own hand. The time to seek ruffs is when you hold two or three low trumps, no use for anything but ruffing. With trump length, you threaten declarer's control of the hand. Make good on that threat by attacking his trumps through a force.

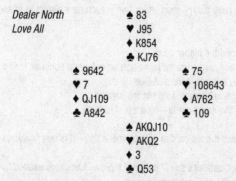

```
Dealer North              ♠ 83
Love All                  ♥ J95
                          ♦ K854
                          ♣ KJ76
      ♠ 9642                           ♠ 75
      ♥ 7                              ♥ 108643
      ♦ QJ109                          ♦ A762
      ♣ A842                           ♣ 109
                          ♠ AKQJ10
                          ♥ AKQ2
                          ♦ 3
                          ♣ Q53
```

Against 4S by South, my partner resisted the singleton heart lead, which declarer would have won, knocked out A♣, and made ten tricks easily.

Instead, he led Q♦, dummy covered and I won with A♦ and returned. Declarer ruffed, and drew two rounds of trumps, discovering the bad break. He now led 3♣, on which West pounced to lead another diamond. Declarer ruffed again, looking mildly nauseous, and, with only one trump left, could not pull West's trumps. When he tried to take heart winners, West could ruff and lead another diamond, using up South's final trump. The defence now came to A♣, A♦, and **two** trump tricks, beating the 4S contract.

Look at the West hand again. Would you have predicted it would make **two** trump tricks?

If you hold four trumps, but no long suit of your own, lead an unbid suit in which your partner will hold length. That way, *he* can force the declarer to ruff, and *your* trumps will be promoted into winning tricks.

His suit – unless you have a very good alternative – such as a singleton in an unbid suit:

- with a doubleton, lead the higher card;
- with three, four or five cards headed by an honour or broken honours, lead a low card – showing interest in the suit (see Tip 92);
- with a sequence of two honours, lead the top honour;
- with three, four, or five small cards – lead top of rubbish.

Don't automatically lead the top card in your partner's suit – it is nearly always wrong.

Consider not leading partner's suit if you have three or four cards headed by the Ace. Leading from the Ace is very dangerous.

Dealer South	♠ AJ3	**N**	**E**	**S**	**W**
E/W Game	♥ 53	–	–	1C	NB
	♦ AQ9854	1D	1H	1NT	NB
	♣ 107	**3NT**			

♠ 98762		♠ 54
♥ K82		♥ AJ1094
♦ J103		♦ 7
♣ J8		♣ A6542

	♠ KQ10
	♥ Q76
	♦ K62
	♣ KQ93

This hand occurred during a friendly teams match in a glamorous Alpine chalet, after a long day's skiing. Both tables reached 3NT after East had overcalled hearts. At my table West – Maria Wiehe – led 2♥ to her partner's A♥. East, Loulou van Geuns, returned J♥, and South's Queen is trapped. Only eight tricks can be made as, when East wins A♣, she has heart winners to defeat the contract.

The board should be flat but, at the second table, West – doubtless still recovering from lunchtime *vin chaud* – led K♥, and now South's Q♥ must score a trick. Game made and a big swing – all on the lead.

Against NT contracts, you always lead your partner's suit, even from the Ace, unless you have a singleton in his suit and a good-quality suit of your own, with entries to enjoy established winners.

Interpreting your partner's lead is essential before you touch your own hand. Following this tip will allow you to make the right decision when the crucial moment presents itself.

These rules apply to leads made at any time during the play of the hand (though, obviously, not right at the end when your choice is severely restricted), as well as to opening leads.

You are often faced with a situation where you would like to lead one suit to partner, but want him to switch and return another. Similarly, have you faced the decision of whether to return partner's suit, or switch to your own? The solutions are simple. Look at the size of the card partner played when he first led the suit, and it will tell you whether he wants us to return the suit, or switch to another.

Dealer South	♠ AQJ		N	E	S	W
N/S Game	♥ 84		–	–	1C	NB
	♦ KQ532		1D	NB	1NT	NB
	♣ 964		3NT			

♠ 107		♠ 6542
♥ 97532		♥ QJ6
♦ 104		♦ A97
♣ A1032		♣ QJ8

	♠ K983
	♥ AK10
	♦ J86
	♣ K75

At the Western Province Trials in Cape Town, South Africa, I was drafted in as a reserve at the last moment, with a partner whom I had never met before. We had one minute to discuss our system: we spent 55 seconds discussing defence …

After a Strong NT auction which led to 3NT, my partner led 7♥, which ran to my J♥ and declarer's K♥. South led 8♦, on which my partner played 4♦, dummy K♦, and I ducked. 2♦ followed and, unwilling to duck again in case declarer had nine tricks, I won. Declarer certainly has enough tricks now, so we must cash winners if we have them. Should I return a heart or find a switch?

Partner's 7♥ could not be low – there were too many lower cards missing – so it must be top of rubbish. Our only chance to defeat the contract lay in attacking clubs; I switched to Q♣ and four tricks there defeated the Game.

During that long evening, playing with a completely new partner, I felt I had played good bridge. We didn't seem to make a costly mistake in 32 deals, only losing narrowly in the final to the South African international team. The key was that both my partner and I made bid and signal clear and simple; if we were in doubt about making an obvious bid or a clever one, we opted for the former. Perhaps this is a lesson to all those players who, like me, love playing lots of gadgets: playing well at a simple level may be more effective than making mistakes at an expert level.

I am accosted by students and friends, in the unlikeliest of places, asking my view on a particular situation (usually, though not exclusively, to do with bridge).

A delightful, but somewhat nervous, student of mine had been reprimanded on this hand, and wanted my view. Despite the fact that we met in a supermarket, and she had me pinned against the loose mushrooms, I studied her diagram:

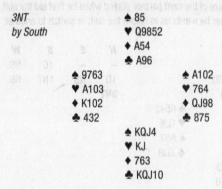

```
3NT             ♠ 85
by South        ♥ Q9852
                ♦ A54
                ♣ A96
       ♠ 9763           ♠ A102
       ♥ A103           ♥ 764
       ♦ K102           ♦ QJ98
       ♣ 432            ♣ 875
                ♠ KQJ4
                ♥ KJ
                ♦ 763
                ♣ KQJ10
```

South was in 3NT after, evidently, a forgettable auction.

'My partner led a spade,' she informed me, 'and I won with A♠. I thought for a bit, led back 10♠, and declarer made it easily.'

Her partner gave her a long lecture as to how it was obvious to switch to a diamond, and that this would have defeated the contract. Apparently, everyone else had agreed.

'What card did your partner lead?'

I was told that West had led 3♠.

It did not surprise me. Those who lecture uninvited have usually made the mistake themselves (except me, of course!) By leading a little spade her partner had promised an honour at the head of the suit, and requested partner win and return spades. She should have led 9♠ to show no interest in the suit. Then, Q♦ looks right.

As it was, declarer could have held ♦K10x and the switch could cost, and partner might have ♠KJ93, and would have been furious if East switched.

Lead thoughtfully; watch partner's lead carefully.

93 / AGAINST SUIT CONTRACTS, NEVER MAKE AN OPENING LEAD AWAY FROM AN ACE – UNLESS THE MUCH GREATER STRENGTH IS ON YOUR LEFT

Leading a little card from a suit headed by an honour is an aggressive move. It risks that declarer can win with an honour lower than your honour – that is a free trick. To lead a little card away from a suit headed by the Ace represents the peak of danger as, not only may declarer win with a lower honour, but he may also be singleton in the suit, and your Ace later gets trumped.

For these reasons, never lead a suit headed by the Ace unless you hold the King also (when you would lead the Ace).

Later during a hand, you may lead from an Ace. If you can see the King on your left (or weakness on your right) then it is safe and you may cause declarer to mis-guess.

Dealer North	♠ A83		N	E	S	W
N/S Game	♥ KJ5		2NT	NB	3S	NB
	♦ AK84		4C	NB	4NT	NB
	♣ AQ6		5C	NB	**6S**	

♠ 94		♠ J5
♥ A7643		♥ Q98
♦ J109		♦ Q7652
♣ 842		♣ 1097

♠ KQ10762
♥ 102
♦ 3
♣ KJ53

As an opening lead, the one time you would consider underleading an Ace was if the bidding confirmed that all the strength was to your left. Then, you might score a psychological coup.

My ultra-aggressive (at bridge) mate, Terry Palmer, visiting from Australia, found this astounding lead:

North can make 6S or 6NT easily, because his dodgy heart position is guarded from attack on the opening lead. 6S by South would make under normal circumstances, but Terry, sitting West, reasoned that it should be safe to lead a little heart from his hand, through dummy's great strength. When declarer saw the 3♥ lead, he concluded that Terry could not underlead A♥ against a Slam, so he called for J♥. I covered with Q♥ and it held the trick. I returned 9♥ and the Slam went down. Needless to say, declarer was apoplectic when he saw the position and close on splenetic when his partner, who had been paying virtually no attention all afternoon, suddenly piped up with the helpful comment:

'If you'd played your K♥ you would have made it.'

Remarkably, not a drop of blood was shed …

94 / NEVER LEAD A DOUBLETON – UNLESS YOUR PARTNER HAS BID

A platinum tip, this one. Because you are leading from weakness around to the strong declarer hand, a doubleton lead often kills your partner's high. Worse still, it usually helps declarer to establish his long suit. Nine times out of ten, leading a doubleton is a bad idea. Leading a doubleton in dummy's bid suit is really bad, and offenders must go and sit in the corner.

Leading a doubleton is a desperately aggressive and dangerous move. To succeed, partner must win and return the suit, and then regain the lead to play it again for your ruff; and all this before declarer has drawn trumps.

The only time such a gambit is worthwhile is when partner has called the suit. I recommend a simple policy of never leading doubletons unless your partner has called the suit. A great by-product of this is that when your partner does lead what appears to be a short suit, you will know it is a singleton.

Dealer North	♠ Q983		N	E	S	W
Love All	♥ KJ5		NB	NB	1H	NB
	♦ J52		1S	NB	2D	NB
	♣ A96		3H	NB	**4H**	
♠ K642		♠ J1075				
♥ 743		♥ Q2				
♦ 93		♦ AQ108				
♣ Q842		♣ J107				
	♠ A					
	♥ A8643					
	♦ K764					
	♣ K53					

This situation is typical of an average social bridge game:

West leads 9♦; East wins A♦ and returns 8♦. Declarer remembers West's high card lead, and runs the trick to dummy's J♦. Afraid of a ruff, declarer spurns the normal trump finesse in favour of drawing two quick rounds, and is delighted when East's Q♥ falls. He now just loses a club on top of A♦.

This whole sorry saga started with that awful doubleton lead: if West leads 2♣ – the unbid suit – he gives nothing away. Declarer takes the heart finesse with dummy's J♥ – and loses. J♣ comes back. Declarer can win and draw the trump, but then must lose two diamond tricks and a club trick, and go down.

Be prepared for partner to notice when, if you had led your doubleton, it would have defeated the contract. Unfortunately partners never spot when by *not* doing the wrong thing, it works out well for you. This is the tragedy of the expert!

95 / DON'T PLAY WITH A TRUMP SUIT IF YOU CAN'T DO ANY TRUMPING

This becomes extra important at Duplicate Pairs, where every last point is vital. However, at Rubber, Teams or Chicago, reaching the correct Game is still crucial.

West	East	East (2)
♠ AK5	♠ Q86	♠ Q743
♥ A853	♥ KQJ7	♥ K762
♦ Q72	♦ J54	♦ 2
♣ A43	♣ Q97	♣ K975

1H	3H
3NT	NB

Following East's limit raise, West correctly re-bids 3NT to show a balanced hand. East, holding no shortages, should realise that there can be no advantage to playing in hearts, since no ruffing can be achieved. He therefore passes the NT Game. As it is, 4H is very unlikely to make and, if it does, 3NT makes the same number of tricks – and that scores more at Duplicate.

If East holds the second hand (2), he responds 3H and, over West's 3NT re-bid, he continues to 4H. With this hand, his singleton diamond is very likely to produce extra tricks through ruffs, and that makes 4H the safer and higher-scoring Game contract.

Here's another classic situation, so often mishandled at the table:

West	East
♠ AKQJ109	♠ 765
♥ A8	♥ Q732
♦ A62	♦ J543
♣ A4	♣ J8

2C	2D
2S	**4S**

When West opens a Game-forcing 2C and then re-bids spades, East may raise to Game weakly, and the contract is likely to fail. Instead, West should re-bid 3NT. He is almost certain that, if he plays in spades, he will be unable to ruff a loser in dummy. So, why have a trump suit?

In fact, West's hand is only worth Game in NTs anyway, so 3NT must be the correct re-bid. If East happens to be strong and bids on, he will not be disappointed to find partner with nine quick tricks.

96 / KEEP AIMING FOR NO-TRUMPS: STOPPER-SHOWING BIDS FOR NO-TRUMP CONTRACTS

This bidding will transform your results; it is essential that you and your partner add it to your system straight away.

Instead of having a minor suit as trumps, your thoughts should always be on trying to play in 3NT. Compared to 5C or 5D, this offers you Game for two less tricks, and extra points if you are scoring for Duplicate Pairs.

Whenever you agree a minor suit, or if one player emphasises a minor suit, any new suit introduced is a Stopper-Showing Bid for no-trumps. Simply, a bid in a new suit tells partner that you have a stopper in that suit, and you need him to name the suit(s) where he has stoppers. Once a player knows that all the suits are covered, he makes a limit bid in no-trumps. Let's see these clever bids in action:

West	East	West	East
♠ A5	♠ 73	1C	3C
♥ 643	♥ KQ8	3D	3H
♦ AQ7	♦ K543	**3NT**	
♣ AQ832	♣ K976		

5C may not make, but 3NT is a certainty. After East agrees clubs, West's 3D bid shows a diamond stopper. East's 3H bid shows a heart stopper. Knowing all suits are covered, West bids 3NT confidently.

West	East	West	East
♠ 5	♠ AK4	1H	2D
♥ AJ853	♥ 62	3D	3S
♦ A754	♦ KQ9832	**3NT**	
♣ AJ8	♣ 74		

When West supports East's diamonds, East investigates the possibility of 3NT by making a Stopper-Showing Bid for no-trumps – his 3S bid. This confirms a stopper in spades and suggests that East is worried about the one unbid suit – clubs. As West has clubs covered, he re-bids 3NT and the best Game is reached.

STOPPER-SHOWING BIDS FOR

West	East	West	East
♠ AK5	♠ QJ4	1C	1H
♥ J6	♥ AK752	3C	3S
♦ 752	♦ 43	4C	5C
♣ AKJ832	♣ Q96		

When East bids 3S over West's strong re-bid, this shows a stopper in spades and, since you show stoppers in ascending order, denies a diamond stopper. As West is without a stopper in diamonds also, he does not bid NTs, but returns to his own long suit where, on this occasion, his side will play.

To use a Stopper-Showing Bid, you must have agreed a minor suit, or emphasised one. You must have sufficient points between you for Game.

Bid your stoppers in the cheapest, or ascending, order. Failure to bid a suit denies a stopper there.

Once one player knows that all suits are covered, he must bid NTs immediately.

If a suit is identified with no stopper between your two hands, play in your minor suit, at the 4 or 5-level.

97 / RE-BID NO-TRUMPS WITH A LONG MINOR, IF UNBID SUITS ARE COVERED

This is a quick but important bidding tip.

♠ 86
♥ K6
♦ AJ3
♣ AKQ986

You open 1D; partner responds 1S. What do you re-bid?

Normally, you might re-bid 3C to show a good six-card suit and about 15–18pts. However, there is a more logical, direct approach: re-bid 3NT.

Your partner has bid spades and you have a stopper in both hearts and diamonds. Even if partner is very weak, with 6–8pts, if clubs divide reasonably, 3NT is quite likely to succeed. The problem is, if partner is very weak, he may pass your 3C re-bid, and nine tricks in clubs are worth considerably less than nine tricks in no-trumps.

When you don't have a stopper in both the unbid suits, you have to make the standard jump re-bid, and then your partner will have to make a Stopper-Showing Bid for NTs, in order to discover if 3NT is still a reasonable proposition.

Not everyone reached a Grand Slam on this hand, from the semi-final stages of the Scottish National Championships, but Peter Hardyment and I quickly, and somewhat precipitously, reached the summit:

West	East	West	East
♠ A5	♠ 874	1C	1H
♥ 6	♥ AKQJ5	3NT	**7NT**
♦ K52	♦ A43		
♣ AKQ10732	♣ J6		

My 3NT re-bid on the West hand ensured that if my partner was minimum, we would be in the best Game. In fact, with 15pts, and expecting me to have the equivalent of 19/20pts, he bid the maximum, and there were 15 potential tricks.

98 / AT RUBBER, TEAMS AND CHICAGO, DON'T DOUBLE THE OPPOSITION FOR PENALTIES IF YOU THINK THAT THEY ARE ONLY GOING ONE DOWN

Why, if you think your opponents may be one down, is doubling a bad bet? The odds are against you: you double your opponents in 4S when they are not vulnerable. If they go one down, you make 100pts, rather than 50pts – a gain of 50pts; if they make it, they gain 120pts and a further 50pts for the insult – a total of 170pts. So, you are risking 170pts to gain 50pts – a bad bet. Double when you *know* your opponents are one off, and you think they will be two or more down.

An old wives' bridge tale which, just for a change, contains a modicum of sense, is that when you double, you should know what you are going to lead.

Dealer South	♠ J	N	E	S	W
Game All	♥ KQJ8	–	–	1C	NB
	♦ KQ75	1H	NB	1S	NB
	♣ Q1076	3NT	NB	4S	NB
		5C	NB	6C	Dbl

♠ 8642		♠ 1053
♥ A743		♥ 109652
♦ A982		♦ J103
♣ A		♣ 98

♠ AKQ97
♥ –
♦ 64
♣ KJ5432

This was a nightmare hand for the defender, Jon Wilson, in the quarter-finals of The Devonshire Cup in the needle match between The Roehampton Club and Queen's Club.

We were down in the match and my partner, Peter Hardyment, sniffed an opportunity, and bid 6C on the South cards, hoping to leave West with a problematic lead decision. Jon Wilson not unreasonably doubled, and we all awaited his lead – for some time ... Eventually, West led the one Ace he knew was winning – A♣ – hoping that dummy would provide inspiration for trick 2. It did not ...

He knew that South held a void somewhere – but where? Jon pulled first one red Ace and then the other. Eventually, he laid down A♥, Peter ruffed and 12 tricks could be made. Only A♦ at trick 2 beats it.

99 / DOUBLE FOR PENALTIES, NOT ON POINTS BUT ON DISTRIBUTION

Many penalty doubles often have a conventional, lead-directing meaning, which can dramatically alter the result of a hand. Generally, social bridge players double for penalties when they have a strong hand – and this is often the wrong time.

If you are playing against decent opposition, their contract will be bid for good reason, particularly after an uninterrupted auction. If you hold a lot of points, you can be fairly certain that your opponents have complementary distribution to make up for any shortfall in high card values.

The correct time to pounce with a penalty double is when both opponents have limited their hands, and you know that the key suits are breaking badly for them.

Dealer North	♠ Q42				**N**	**E**	**S**	**W**
E/W Game	♥ KJ842				1H	NB	1S	NB
	♦ AK75				2S	NB	3S	NB
	♣ 6				4S	NB	NB	Dbl
♠ J10985		♠ –						
♥ 5		♥ AQ107						
♦ 982		♦ QJ63						
♣ A874		♣ QJ953						
	♠ AK763							
	♥ 963							
	♦ 104							
	♣ K102							

North-South meander into 4S – ostensibly, not a terrible contract, but the opponents' distribution dooms it to a disastrous fate. West must double, not simply because of his five trumps and A♣, but because, from the bidding, he knows that N/S are tight on points and that his partner must hold hearts over the opener. This means that there is no side-suit South can establish for discards. Decent defence nets six tricks and N/S lose 500pts.

An additional factor was that West's trumps were solid. Even if his double tips South off to the bad split, there's nothing declarer can do about it. Doubling with broken honours is dangerous, as declarer's play may improve with the information you have provided him.

100 / DON'T EAT CRUDITÉS AT THE BRIDGE TABLE

I'm a big fan of a drink and some canapés at the bridge table. If you are going to play social bridge, it should be sociable. I draw the line at food that drips or spatters after seeing a player eating runny fried eggs and bacon whilst trying to perform a complex squeeze in 6S doubled: he didn't make it; neither did the eggs, dribbling down his shirt in a dayglow yellow trail. I won't even tell you where his bacon came to rest!

A while back, one of my private bridge classes featured four ladies of a certain age, and a large unruly German Shepherd. One afternoon, the ladies decided to break for tea and we all sat down to Earl Grey and an impressive Victoria Sponge. Unbeknownst to us, a large chunk ended up in the lap of a tall, dignified lady. Later, just as she was peering over her pince-nez at dummy, the aforementioned hound sauntered casually into the room, under the table, and stuck its nose into the declarer's skirt. She, the table, my set hand, and her cup of tea all went flying as hysteria broke out.

The last straw came the evening my partner became so engrossed in the defence to a 3NT contract that she dunked her cards into the blue-cheese dip instead of the cauliflower floret in her other hand. Thankfully, the story had a happy ending: the deal had to be abandoned, and the opponents would have made their contract.

101 / INTRODUCING THE 'PUDDING RAISE'

In the old days, if you could support partner's major suit and you had a strong hand, you made a Delayed Game Raise – changing suit first, then raising to Game subsequently. Nowadays, it is an integral part of modern Acol – and many other systems – that if you hold four-card support for partner's major suit, you must support him immediately. To that end, you may require a new bid – and that is where the 'Pudding Raise' comes in.

West	East	West	East
♠ AQ952	♠ K874	1S	?
♥ 6	♥ AQ4		
♦ AK52	♦ J7		
♣ J87	♣ A632		

East must support spades immediately, but the limit raises all show weaker hands: 1S-2S shows 6–9pts; 1S-3S shows 10–12pts; and 1S-4S denies more than 9pts.

You need a bid that shows four-card spade support with 13–16pts – and that bid should be a direct response of 3NT.

No decent player would jump all the way to 3NT with any old balanced opening hand, since it makes sense to respond quietly and listen to partner's re-bid before deciding in which denomination to play. However, here, since you know that spades will be trumps, the direct response of 3NT shows four-card support or better, 13–16pts, and no singletons or voids. This is why it is called a 'Pudding Raise' – it is flat and stodgy.

Almost always, opener will convert to the major suit at the 4-level, or look for a Slam. Occasionally, if opener has a completely flat 15/16pts, with only a four-card major, he may pass 3NT – after all, why have a trump suit if you can't trump anywhere?

The 'Pudding Raise' is a response which can be used over any opening bid at the 1-level – major or minor. If it is the latter, responder must show any four-card major suit at the 1-level initially. If he does respond 3NT, opener is far more likely to pass this as, with a fit in a minor suit, 3NT is the preferred contract.

Unless you have more advanced methods – of which there are many – I recommend discussing this bid with your partner and including it in your system immediately.

102 / 'SPLINTER BIDS' PINPOINT PERFECT DISTRIBUTION

'Splinter Bids' are a gadget to be added to your system to increase your descriptive abilities. They are cousins of the 'Pudding Raise' in the previous tip. To keep things simple, we will look at the occasions they are most useful: in response to partner's opening bid of 1H or 1S, and as opener's re-bid when partner's response has been 1H, 2H or 1S.

In response to an opening bid, a response in a new suit at the third available level is a 'Splinter' – showing four-card support for partner's major suit, 10–15pts and a singleton or void in the suit bid. NB – this jump cannot be a pre-empt; you *never* pre-empt in a new suit after your partner has bid.

West	East	West	East
♠ 4	♠ AJ87	1H	4D
♥ AQJ864	♥ K953	4NT	5H
♦ 752	♦ 3	**6H**	
♣ AK3	♣ QJ62		

East's response of 4D is a 'Splinter' showing four-card heart support, 10–15pts, and a singleton or void in diamonds. Despite holding only 14pts, West is excited about the prospect of a Slam, because partner's shortage means that he will not lose more than one diamond, and that East's points must be in spades, hearts and clubs. He uses Roman Key-Card Blackwood to check that he is not missing too many control cards, and then he bids 6H confidently.

If West had been unimpressed by East's singleton diamond, he simply returns to 4H.

As an opener's re-bid, the 'Splinter' takes place just below the Game level, and shows sufficient points, including distribution, to make Game viable. Over a 1-level response, opener will need the equivalent of 19/20pts; over a 2-level response, 17–20pts.

West	East	West	East
♠ AKQ95	♠ J4	1S	2H
♥ QJ97	♥ A8532	4C	4H
♦ AJ7	♦ 843		
♣ 2	♣ KJ6		

Here, West re-bids 4C to show a raise to Game, four-card heart support and a singleton or void in clubs. East is not interested: he is minimum, holds values in clubs, and lousy cards in diamonds and spades. He signs off in 4H, a decision which West must respect.

If your opponents bid, you may only Splinter in their suit, to show a singleton or void, four-card support for your partner's major suit, and Game-going values. Jumps in other suits are not played as Splinters, but have a different meaning.

103 / WITH A LONG MINOR SUIT, ALWAYS SUPPORT NTS

If you have been reading this book chronologically, I suspect that you will have spotted a recurring theme: playing in a NT contract when you have a minor suit. In case you have flipped to this tip out of the blue, or if you are a less-experienced player, this is truly a platinum tip.

Your partner opens 1NT (12–14). What do you respond?

♠ Q9
♥ J7
♦ 854
♣ AKJ974

I recommend 3NT. Your partner's points are in spades, hearts and diamonds, and he will love your long club suit, which should produce six tricks. Do not bid 3C. Some people play this as a Slam try, some to show a very weak hand. No one bids 3C with the hand shown, because 3NT is definitely the right bid.

The reason it is right is because, if you want to try for Game, 5C requires way too many tricks. You won't make 3NT every time but, in the long run, you will get rich.

Bonus Tip!
Your partner opens 1NT again. What do you respond this time?

♠ 3
♥ 42
♦ AQ954
♣ AQJ74

I recommend 3NT again. 5C or 5D might make, but 3NT is still the most likely Game contract. More importantly, unless you play an advanced system, the bidding will never be able to tell you the best spot. Partner is likely to have a stopper in both majors, and at least one of your minor suits will produce five quick tricks. Nine tricks should come home.

So, **with two long minor suits, support NTs.**

104 / RESPONDER'S RE-BIDS SHOW SIX-CARD SUITS

Once opener has described his hand with his initial bid and re-bid, responder has to decide how to proceed.

With weak hands, generally containing 6–10pts, responder will probably show preference between opener's two suits, or bid 1NT, and sometimes 2NT.

With stronger hands, say 11pts+, responder may jump to Game, or use Fourth Suit Forcing.

On the cusp of these two bids lies responder's re-bid of his own suit. Because he is ignoring opener's suits and not bidding or investigating a NT contract, he is likely to hold most of his values in his suit – and that suit will always contain six cards or more:

West	East	West	East
♠ 4	♠ KQ9865	1H	1S
♥ AQJ95	♥ 8	2C	2S
♦ Q52	♦ 964	NB	
♣ KQ86	♣ A53		

When East responds 2S, he promises a six-card suit of decent quality and about 8–10pts. If West holds a singleton or void spade, he passes, and leaves the contract at the 2-level. If he holds a top doubleton honour, or three-card support, he may raise to 3S or 4S.

If you play Fourth Suit Forcing, responder's jump re-bid is not forcing, because to create a forcing situation, you should first bid the fourth suit and then re-bid your own six-card suit.

However, if you do not play Fourth Suit Forcing, then it would be logical to play responder's jump re-bid as forcing, so that you cannot miss Game.

West	East	West	East
♠ 95	♠ J4	1D	1H
♥ Q7	♥ AKJ532	2C	3H
♦ AJ864	♦ K7	**4H**	
♣ AK85	♣ 963		

Despite holding 12pts, if opener has a singleton heart, Game may well not be available, so 3H (played as non-forcing) seems right on hands of 11/12pts. Here, West's hand is very suitable; he holds Q♥, and Ace-King and another Ace. It should be easy for West to raise to Game.

With any hand stronger than this, use Fourth Suit Forcing first, and then plan to re-bid your hearts over opener's third bid. This establishes a Game-forcing situation.

105 / AVOID OVERCALLS IN THE SANDWICH POSITION

What with 'Pudding Raises' and the 'sandwich position', this section is turning out to be quite food orientated. I use this term here to remind you how dangerous it is to overcall when your opponents have unlimited strength and have yet to find a fit. The purpose of an overcall is to obstruct, but you must obstruct early – before your opponents have described their hands – otherwise, the effect is limited and the chances of you being doubled for penalties are greatly increased.

This hand cropped up in an Australian event, where my partner and I took advantage of our opponent's poor timing:

Dealer North	♠ A8532	**N**	**E**	**S**	**W**
Game All	♥ KJ84	1S	NB	2D	2H
	♦ A75	NB	NB	Dbl	
	♣ 6				

♠ KQ6	♠ J1097
♥ AQ10753	♥ 9
♦ 92	♦ QJ8
♣ K9	♣ J10743

♠ 4
♥ 62
♦ K10643
♣ AQ852

West's 2H looks justified: he has 14pts and a good-quality six-card suit, but he is sandwiched between unlimited hands who, crucially, have not found a fit. If your opponents don't have a fit, neither will you – and West found out the hard way.

Sitting North, I passed over West's 2H bid to show a minimum opener, and my partner re-opened with a take-out double. Since Game in diamonds looks a long way off, and my hand seems unsuitable for no-trumps, I converted the double to penalties and set about defending. We managed the first nine tricks and collected a penalty of +1100pts. And what could we make? Nothing; maybe 2NT or 3D, but no Game.

The principle is that South's 2D is forcing and West should wait until he hears North and South's re-bids, before deciding whether to risk the overcall.

At the table, West muttered something about his bid being lead-directing, but the odds are that East would find a heart lead anyway.

106 / IF YOU MUST GUESS, SET A SNARE

A two-way finesse should not be a guess; the bidding or play preceding it should help you to make the right decision. Sometimes, however, when it is the trump-suit in which you face the decision, you may have to play it early on. You are, effectively, committed to guessing the position of the missing honour. However, against average bridge players, you can set a snare, which may make the decision for you.

Dealer East	♠ A85		N	E	S	W
E/W Game	♥ K63		–	NB	1H	NB
	♦ AK52		2D	NB	2H	NB
	♣ 764		4H			

	♠ J1097		♠ 642
	♥ Q74		♥ 85
	♦ 1063		♦ QJ98
	♣ AJ8		♣ K1095

	♠ KQ3
	♥ AJ1092
	♦ 74
	♣ Q32

West leads J♠ against South's 4H contract, and declarer decides that he has three certain club losers, so must avoid loss in hearts. How should he play the suit?

It's unlikely that playing other suits first will enlighten him as to where Q♥ is located, so the trumps should be tackled immediately. With no evidence from bidding or play, it is just a guess. However, since you hold ♥J109 in the hidden hand, by leading J♥ you can tempt West to cover it. If he does – or if he pauses to think about it – you've discovered where the Queen lies. If West follows small without a flicker, you can assume that West does not hold the Queen. Now, you overtake J♥ with dummy's K♥, and take the finesse through the East hand.

If West deliberately hesitates when he holds only small cards, that is cheating.

This won't work against decent players. West should know already that East holds two hearts at most. That means that West cannot promote a trick in East's hand, and it can never be right to cover South's honour. However, an unwary defender may not have anticipated the J♥ lead and will give away the position of Q♥. When this hand was first played, West covered South's J♥ and the hand was over almost instantly.

107 / DISCUSS PART-SCORE SITUATIONS WITH PARTNER – AND SOLVE THE PROBLEM BEFORE IT ARISES

There is little more frustrating at Rubber bridge than to miss a Slam because you were not certain if your partner was bidding to the score or not. Come to that, it's pretty galling to get too high when all you needed was 40pts.

I recommend agreeing a simple policy when your side holds a part-score:

- With *Slam-going* hands, jump-shift immediately. Partner is forced to continue bidding at least until Game.
- With an *opening* hand, support partner to one level above necessary to score Game. This shows that you are not averse to seeking a Slam if partner holds a maximum opener.
- With *weaker* hands, agree a suit at the minimum level required to give you Game.

Although this is a relatively rigid system, it is simple to explain and will boost your partnership confidence.

Dealer South	♠ A8		
N/S 60p/s	♥ QJ83		
	♦ KQ75		
	♣ 763		

N	E	S	W
–	–	1H	2C
3H	NB	4NT	NB
5D	NB	6H	

♠ 642		♠ J1053
♥ 76		♥ 92
♦ 82		♦ 9643
♣ AKQ842		♣ J95

♠ KQ97
♥ AK1054
♦ AJ10
♣ 10

As West, my 2C overcall was pretty horrible, but I'm not sure I could have put N/S off their Slam.

My dear Cape Town friends, Kate and Lindsay Birch, made me pay for my timid approach. With 60pts below the line already, Lindsay's jump to 3H showed an opening hand. After this, her strong hand and singleton club persuaded Kate to wade into Blackwood and bid the unbeatable Slam.

Had Lindsay bid just to the score, with a raise to 2H, the Slam would have been missed.

108 / BID UP AT RUBBER AND CHICAGO – IT'S THE ONLY WAY TO WIN

Like most card games, there is a right and wrong style in which to play, and the winning gambits are those that play the odds. If you play poker or blackjack, you may get a 'feeling' for what to do but, unless it is in line with the odds, it will lose in the long run. A famous blackjack professional told me that when he comes across students of the game who say they have a sixth sense, he tells them:

'That's great. You're not just another mug – you're a mug with a hunch!'

At the highest level, every bridge decision is based on all the information available at that moment. Experts spend time calculating the odds of many plays before committing themselves.

At a social or club level, it is best to stick to a basic strategy. Bonuses for winning the rubber, or Chicago game bonuses, are so great, you should bid quite optimistic Game contracts, certainly relying on a finesse, or even worse.

a	*b*
♠ AQ5432	♠ A8753
♥ 76	♥ 2
♦ KJ98	♦ A96
♣ 6	♣ AJ108

In both cases, you open 1S and partner responds 3S (10–12pts, four-card support). Should you bid 4S?

a) Yes. You may be minimum, but now that you have 10 of them, your spade quality no longer matters. Your shape and extra length make bidding 4S clear-cut.
b) Yes. 5-4-3-1 hands often play well and, if your partner has some values in clubs or diamonds, you should succeed. It is definitely worth a go.

In both cases, you cannot discover whether partner holds the cards you seek, but the Game bonus is so great, you must risk bidding Game.

The vulnerability is unimportant. I frequently hear people whining, 'I would have bid it if we hadn't been vulnerable …' This is a terrible excuse. When vulnerable you'll make a bigger bonus; you should be even keener to bid up. Vulnerability is really only significant in competitive auctions.

Perhaps you bid 4S on both these hands anyway. If so, bravo! I bet you're a winner.

109 / KEEP YOUR ENTRY SAFE WHEN ESTABLISHING A SUIT IN NO-TRUMPS

This tip applies to both declarer and defenders, but here it is the latter on whom the spotlight falls. To keep an entry in an outside suit is important but, if you don't have one, the entry must be maintained in the suit you are leading:

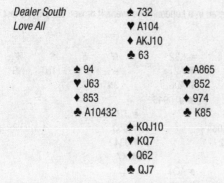

Dealer South
Love All

North:
♠ 732
♥ A104
♦ AKJ10
♣ 63

West:
♠ 94
♥ J63
♦ 853
♣ A10432

East:
♠ A865
♥ 852
♦ 974
♣ K85

South:
♠ KQJ10
♥ KQ7
♦ Q62
♣ QJ7

South plays in 3NT; West leads 3♣ to East's K♣, and East returns 8♣ to declarer's Q♣. What should West do?

If West wins this trick, he can clear the club suit but, as he has no entry, he will never be able to enjoy his winners. His partner, however, surely holds an entry. So, West must duck this trick to keep his A♣ and, more importantly, to maximise the chance that East still has a club left to return when he gains the lead.

If West ducks, South can take eight tricks, but will have to play on spades sooner or later. East leaps in immediately, returns 5♣, and West's three tricks defeat the contract.

110 / THE LEADER'S PARTNER MUST BE READY TO PERFORM HIS VITAL ROLE

In many No-Trump defences, the partner of the leader has one very important role: to gain the lead as soon as possible, and return the suit originally led by his partner. This is so that the hand with the long suit preserves his entries until he has tricks ready to cash.

When this hand appeared in a London Pairs event, it proved too great a test for many East players.

Dealer South	♠ K32		N	E	S	W
Game All	♥ A2		–	–	1NT	NB
	♦ AQ6		3NT			
	♣ J10943					

	♠ 94		♠ J10865
	♥ QJ1064		♥ 953
	♦ 8532		♦ J94
	♣ A6		♣ K7

	♠ AQ4
	♥ K87
	♦ K107
	♣ Q852

West led Q♥ against South's 3NT contract. Declarer has only eight tricks and must attack clubs for extra ones. Most declarers won in dummy with A♥, and led 3♣. At many tables, East played low and West won with A♣. Some Wests even ducked and, on the next round, A♣ and K♣ crashed!

When West did win, he led another heart, and declarer ducked, winning the third heart led. Now, when East wins his K♣, he has no hearts to lead and the contract makes.

If East follows this tip, he will know to rise immediately with K♣; if declarer had better clubs, he would have finessed the King anyway – it is dead meat. When K♣ holds the trick, East fires back 9♥. Whether declarer ducks or wins, when West takes his A♣, his hearts are established and he can defeat the contract.

111 / SECOND HAND DOES NOT ALWAYS PLAY LOW

You've just seen a prime example of this in Tip 110. Here's another one, made for vital, logical reasons. To ensure your best chance of defeating your opponents' contracts, be on the look-out for these situations at the table.

Dealer North	♠ 42		N	E	S	W
N/S Game	♥ 642		–	–	2NT	NB
	♦ AJ1082		3NT			
	♣ 987					

	♠ J975	♠ 1086
	♥ J10987	♥ Q53
	♦ K4	♦ Q93
	♣ Q3	♣ KJ105

	♠ AKQ3
	♥ AK
	♦ 765
	♣ A642

N/S reach 3NT and, once West has led J♥, he notices that dummy contains a threatening diamond suit, but without an outside entry. Both East and West should now be focused on sealing the declarer off from this long suit. East overtakes with Q♥ and declarer wins in hand. He now leads 5♦ – what should West do?

The basic, general rule, that second hand to play, plays low, is just that – a general background rule. There are plenty of times when it is not correct, and this is one of them. If West lazily plays his 4♦, declarer finesses with J♦, and East wins with Q♦.* Now, when South regains the lead, and plays another diamond, West's Queen appears and dummy scores four diamond tricks, allowing declarer to record an overtrick.

If West is focused on severing declarer's communications with dummy, he rises with his K♦! Look at the effect this has on South. If he wins A♦ and plays a second diamond, East ducks, and the suit is nullified; if South ducks K♦, West leads 10♥ to knock out South's last heart stopper, and when East takes his Q♦, he returns a heart to defeat the contract. Once again, if South holds Q♦, West's K♦ is a dead duck anyway, so it cannot cost to insert the honour at this point. This kind of defence crops up far more regularly than one might think and, if you can defeat these contracts, your scores will improve significantly.

If East craftily ducks, declarer can prevail by playing a low diamond from dummy, dropping West's K♦. Later, when he plays to A♦, East's Q♦ drops, and the suit is good.

112 / A DOUBLE OF A FREELY BID SLAM ASKS FOR AN UNUSUAL LEAD

Since it is unlikely that a decent pair will bid a Slam missing two cashable Aces, or Ace-King of a suit, to double a freely bid Slam asks for an unusual lead; usually because you have a void. Partner must work out where it is and find the killing lead. This bid is called a 'Lightner' double – and it can transform a making Slam for your opponents into a penalty for your side.

This deal helped to swing a crucial match in my team's favour at a recent multiple teams event in Cape Town, South Africa:

```
Dealer North      ♠ 2                              N     E     S     W
N/S Game          ♥ AJ                             1D    3S    4C    NB
                  ♦ AK8543                         4NT   NB    5D    NB
                  ♣ KQ85                           6C    Dbl

        ♠ Q86                  ♠ AJ109753
        ♥ 9876532              ♥ –
        ♦ J6                   ♦ 1092
        ♣ 10                   ♣ 973

                  ♠ K4
                  ♥ KQ104
                  ♦ Q7
                  ♣ AJ642
```

At the other table, 6C was also the contract, but it was played by North. East led A♠ and that was the defence's only trick. At my table, South bid clubs directly over my 3S pre-emptive overcall and when, via Blackwood, North bid the Slam, I doubled for an unusual lead. Partner led 9♥ and I ruffed, before cashing A♠: +200 to us, instead of -1370.

There is a footnote, however, and that is that South can redeem the situation easily enough, by converting 6C doubled to 6NT, in which 12 tricks are certain.

That got me thinking: if I hadn't doubled, would West have still led a heart against 6C? He wouldn't, he told me. 'If you don't double, you can't have a heart void … so I lead a spade and 6C makes anyway.'

113 / TO OPEN, HAVE 12 HIGH-CARD POINTS – OR A SIX-CARD SUIT

This simple advice will help your side to avoid over-bidding. With few exceptions this is my policy, even when playing at the top level.

If you open the bidding with 10 or 11pts and a five-card suit, or even two five-card suits, you often end up in unmakable Games and Slams. A six-card suit is massively more powerful than a five-card suit, and that is why you can open light with a six-card suit. Obviously, there are also weak pre-empts with a seven-card suit, and Weak Two openers with terrible hands containing a decent six-card suit.

a	*b*	*c*	*d*
♠ J2	♠ –	♠ AQJ87	♠ KQJ987
♥ K6	♥ J8542	♥ KJ985	♥ 6
♦ AJ32	♦ AK4	♦ 54	♦ A95
♣ Q9764	♣ K7532	♣ 3	♣ 843

a) Pass. You have lousy suits and your partner will only be disappointed if you open the bidding. Even worse, when your partner responds a major suit, you cannot re-bid 2D, as this would be a reverse, showing 16pts+.

b) Pass. Again, your suits are horrible. The opponents are likely to compete aggressively in spades, and your partner may misjudge his actions. If you pass and your opponents bid and show weakness, you can re-enter the auction with a take-out double or an unusual NT overcall.

c) 1S. This is the exception. All your points are in your long major suits and you have no re-bid problems whatsoever.

d) 1S. Definitely worth an opening bid. Your six-card suit improves your hand enormously, and all your points are working.

Some aggressive players swear by ultra-light opening bids, but I have never found that a 1-level opening by my opponent affects my judgement, so the pre-emptive argument is lost immediately. Indeed, if I end up playing, I now have a better idea of where the outstanding points are located. The logical policy is to be ultra-aggressive with pre-empts, and raising partner's overcalls, but keep 1-level openers up to strength.

This is not basic advice to beginners; this is for experienced players.

What do you open on this hand?

♠ AQ
♥ AJ
♦ J986
♣ J7632

Playing a Strong NT, it's easy: open 1C and re-bid 1NT. Playing a Weak NT, it is more difficult. If you open 1C, and partner responds, say, 1H – what can you re-bid now? 2D is a reverse, showing 16pts+; if you re-bid 2C, you have emphasised a truly lousy suit.

Since all possible re-bids are so bad, opt instead to open 1NT. Your hand is not completely balanced, but you have good cards in your short suits and the correct point-count. More importantly, you've described your hand decently in one bid, leaving your partner to make a decision about the final contract.

What about this one?

♠ A
♥ AKQJ1064
♦ 8432
♣ A

If you open 1H, or a Strong 2H, you risk missing Game if partner passes. If you open 2C (Game-forcing) and re-bid hearts, you'll end up in the wrong contract. With nine certain tricks, you do have Game in your own hand, but only in 3NT – and that is how you should plan to describe your hand.

This cropped up in a Duplicate event, and the traveller made for fascinating reading. Contracts ranged from 1H to 5H, but my partnership played in 3NT. I opened 2C and, over partner's complete negative response of 2H (we play a slightly different method of responding to 2C), I re-bid 3NT. There we played, making nine tricks. Here are both hands:

West	East
♠ A	♠ J7532
♥ AKQJ1064	♥ 85
♦ 8432	♦ J7
♣ A	♣ 9654

Even if my opponents had led diamonds, they would only have made four tricks. As it was, North led a club, and I took my nine tricks happily. In 4H, it was easy enough for N/S to pull dummy's trumps before West could ruff a diamond, and he goes on to make the same nine tricks – one down.

As with all contracts at Duplicate Pairs, you are seeking to make the biggest plus score possible (or the smallest minus score) and, at the Slam level, attention to this detail can bring you an armful of match-points.

Playing with one of my students, this deal scored us 98% of the match-points in a UK County Pairs event:

Dealer South	♠ K865		**N**	**E**	**S**	**W**
N/S Game	♥ A754		–	–	1S	NB
	♦ A8		3S	NB	4C	NB
	♣ 9742		4D	NB	4NT	NB
♠ QJ		♠ 10	5C	NB	**6NT**	
♥ Q1093		♥ KJ862				
♦ 1095		♦ 6432				
♣ K652		♣ J108				
	♠ A97432					
	♥ –					
	♦ KQJ7					
	♣ AQ3					

Over North's limit raise to 3S, I was pretty convinced that I would play in 6S. However, if partner holds K♠, A♦ and K♣, 7S will be good and, if he holds his actual hand, 6NT will score better. Some further investigation is required.

4C is a cue-bid, showing A♣; 4D shows A♦. Now, when Roman Key-Card Blackwood told me that partner held three key-cards, I know that 12 tricks must be available in 6NT and that, having bid only 3S, partner cannot also hold K♣.

The traveller showed most pairs in 6S; some bid 7S, some missed the Slam altogether. Only one other pair bid 6NT and we shared a top with them.

So, at the 6-level, your general thought should be to play in a major rather than a minor suit and in no-trumps rather than the major suit.

If you find that a Grand Slam seems likely then, unless you are playing in a very strong field, merely bidding the grand will gain you most of the match-points – denomination becomes much less important. If 7C seems more likely to make than 7NT, settle for the minor suit Grand Slam. There will be plenty who will play in only 6C, or feel that they have done enough trying 6NT.

116 / USE QUANTITATIVE RAISES TO BID NO-TRUMP SLAMS

If you think you might bid 6NT, often you don't need Blackwood. Instead, rely on arithmetic to get there. One of the best gadgets to help you is a Quantitative Raise. With relatively balanced hands, to make 6NT you require a combined point-count of 33/34pts. When you are in doubt that your side has this total, you can find out quickly and easily.

West	East	West	East
♠ K86	♠ Q7	1NT	4NT
♥ QJ95	♥ AK7	**6NT**	
♦ KJ86	♦ A94		
♣ A4	♣ KQJ85		

When West opens 1NT (12–14), East knows that his side hold 31–33pts. If West is minimum, E/W are unlikely to have sufficient values to make 12 tricks, whereas if West is maximum, the combined point-count is correct. To discover this, East simply raises to 4NT.

When your partner's last bid is a natural NT bid, if you bid 4NT, it is *not* Blackwood of any kind – it is a Quantitative Raise. This is logical, since you have not agreed a suit.

If opener is minimum for his NT bid, he passes 4NT; if he is maximum, he raises to 6NT.

Note that, if you hold 33/34pts between you, you cannot be missing two Aces.

If you know that your side holds 33/34pts even if partner is minimum for his NT bid, bid 6NT directly, and do not use a Quantitative Raise.

This second situation is ideal for a Quantitative Raise, since the range of NT re-bid is so wide:

West	East	West	East
♠ K74	♠ 965	1D	2C
♥ KJ7	♥ AQ4	3NT	4NT
♦ AQJ86	♦ K9	**6NT**	
♣ AJ	♣ KQ874		

In modern Acol, over a 2-level response, West's 3NT re-bid shows 17–20pts. East calculates that if West is minimum, they are short for 6NT but, if West is maximum, they will have the combined 33/34pts. Again, 4NT is not Blackwood, but Quantitative. West is maximum, and bids the excellent Slam.

There are other opportunities to use Quantitative Raises, and at other levels, but they scarcely ever come up.

117 / THREE MINI-TIPS FOR SUCCESSFUL DUPLICATE PLAY

Here are three quick tips. They are basic, but usually ignored by most players.

1 Don't play conventions and gadgets that you don't fully understand

If you do, you will give away match-points every time the gadget crops up. I know very modest players who claim to play every convention under the sun. Unfortunately, they play them all badly.

You know how to make a Transfer: do you know the meanings of all the re-bids? You play Weak Twos: are you sure you are fluent in every response and re-bid?

Check with your partner on all your gadgets or agree not to play them. I guarantee a less stressful, more successful session.

2 Assess the value of every contract, all the time

Duplicate Pairs is all about scoring the biggest plus score, or the smallest minus score, on every single hand. Each deal, you must be aware of what your side stands to gain or lose, and decide if another bid might not improve your plus score, or lessen your minus score. Only by doing this will you ever know when to compete, how aggressive to be, how to judge sacrifices, when to double and when to remain quiet.

Note the vulnerability at the outset and keep asking yourself questions.

By the way, when I see a player look on the back of a bidding card to work out the score, I know that they can't be very good: to be successful, you must know – or be able to work out – the scores.

3 Your attitude at the table is worth match-points to you

In his older years, my most frequent partner has mellowed from intolerable bully to a slightly more pleasant, still ambitious, only moderately insulting partner.

For years, opponents came to our table to hear him berating me for whatever hadn't taken his fancy on the previous deal. A few years back, at the final of the Scottish National Pairs, I asked him to pretend that he was happy with his partner, and to appear confident at the table – just for once … He managed it most of the long, close final and, when we won, he churlishly admitted that maybe it had contributed. I am certain of it.

When you arrive at a new table, compliment your partner casually on something from the previous round. If your opponents ask you how you are doing, tell them positively that you are scoring well. Often opponents don't like hearing this; sometimes, you hear them mutter something like: 'I don't like the sound of this.'

Duplicate bridge players aren't used to hearing opponents tell them that they are happy and doing well. Surprise them.

Lastly, when you leave the table, encourage your opponents. The better they play in all future rounds, the more it benefits you, because they are playing against all your opponents sitting in the same direction as you. You want them to do well.

You may be surprised just how far a little psychology takes you!

118 / YOUR OPPONENTS DO NOT KNOW WHAT YOU HAVE IN YOUR HAND; DON'T TELL THEM

Impossible contracts sometimes make – usually because the defenders do not know that declarer cannot possibly make his contract. They panic, and help him. As declarer, when you face an 'unmakable' contract, do your best to induce help from your opponents; you'd be surprised how often they seem to want to help!

		N	E	S	W
Dealer East	♠ J52	**N**	**E**	**S**	**W**
N/S Game	♥ AQ10	–	NB	1C	NB
	♦ 863	3C	NB	**3NT**	
	♣ K1097				

```
            ♠ J52
            ♥ AQ10
            ♦ 863
            ♣ K1097
♠ A96                    ♠ K1084
♥ J8752                  ♥ 64
♦ Q95                    ♦ KJ74
♣ J5                     ♣ 862
            ♠ Q73
            ♥ K93
            ♦ A102
            ♣ AQ43
```

This deal featured in a charity pairs event. Almost everyone played in 3NT, but no one should have made it. My partner succeeded by inducing assistance from West.

West leads 5♥, and South counts eight tricks. Unfortunately, the spade suit is frozen: if declarer plays it, he is unlikely to score a trick; if his opponents lead it, he must win one.

South played Q♥ from dummy, ensuring that West now knows that East does not hold ♥K. Now, he leads 3♦, and he finesses with his 10♦. It's not a finesse, of course, but it looks like one. West wins Q♦, and now what does he think? The hearts are dead, clubs have been agreed, and declarer seems to be establishing diamonds. Looks like the only hope for the defence lies in spades. So, West switches promptly to a spade, and South waits to collect his ninth trick in comfort.

These swindles don't always work but, when they do, it's doubly satisfying: a made Game contract and humiliated opponents – what's not to like?

119 / REMAIN ALERT, HOWEVER POOR YOUR HAND

At Duplicate Pairs, you should remain alert at all times, since whatever cards you hold will be held by every other player sitting in the same position. Your duty is to make one trick more with your rubbish than anybody else.

At Rubber or Chicago, a run of bad cards can be depressing and costly, but top players still rise to the occasion however awful their hand.

My partner, Sajid Ispahani – sitting with a perfect Yarborough – made a careless declarer pay dearly.

Against South's 4S contract, I led ♣AKQ, and declarer strangely declined to ruff the third round, instead discarding 2♦. A trump trick now seems the best hope, so I led a fourth club. Dummy ruffed with 7♠: what should Sajid – sitting East – do now?

If he had over-ruffed, South could over-ruff himself, cash ♥AK and ruff a heart in dummy. With the suit established, he draws trumps and makes his contract. Saj, however, thought more deeply. If South requires a heart ruff, he will be unable to draw all the trumps. East therefore decided to pitch 2♥ – and now, when South tries to ruff the third round, he gets over-ruffed by East, and 4S is defeated.

120 / ANTICIPATE WHAT CONTRACT YOUR OPPONENTS MIGHT MAKE – THEN, STOP THEM!

Occasionally, there are times at the table when you know exactly what contract your opponents might make – and it is more than you can bid. To stop them, consider making an advanced sacrifice, hoping to play there undoubled or, at the very least, to use up as much bidding space as possible, so making it far harder for your opponents to judge what to do.

Your partner opens 1NT (12–14), and your RHO passes. What response do you make?

> ♠ 7
> ♥ 9765432
> ♦ 6543
> ♣ 9

To pass here would be quite wrong. The normal bid would be to make a weak take-out into 2H, either bidding it directly, or by using a transfer. The problem with this is that your opponents will then find it easy to bid their 4S contract – and you know that they are making it! Let's see how:

Partner holds a maximum of 14pts, and you hold none. This gives your opponents 26–28pts between them; clearly Game values. Almost no one opens 1NT with a five-card major suit, so partner is marked with a four-card spade suit at most, indicating that your opponents hold at least an eight-card fit there. 4S seems rock solid for them.

If you bid 4H directly, it may well be passed out, and you will play there, undoubled, probably for one or two down. Even if you get doubled, it is a safe contract. If your opponents bid on, they will either have to have a very strong hand, or nerves of steel to enter the auction. This was the full deal:

		♠ K642	**N**	**E**	**S**	**W**
		♥ KQ8			1NT	NB	4H	?
		♦ A2				
		♣ Q852				

♠ QJ953		♠ A108
♥ A		♥ J10
♦ K97		♦ QJ108
♣ AJ73		♣ K1064

	♠ 7	
	♥ 9765432	
	♦ 6543	
	♣ 9	

It is tough to think what West might bid. Vulnerable, any action is very risky. Whilst a take-out double is more flexible, to over-call 4S directly is probably best, ensuring that you find your 5-3 spade fit if it exists. Indeed, the quicker my opponents bid 4H, the keener I am to risk 4S – it is very often correct.

In a teams match, one South player responded 2H, as a Weak Take-out, and East-West reached 4S easily, and made it with an overtrick. At the other table, South responded 4H and, after some thought, both East and West passed. 4H failed by one trick and a significant swing was achieved for the more imaginative South.

121 / SOCIAL BRIDGE EVENINGS – KEY INFORMATION

Depending upon your temperament and, to some extent, on your prowess at the game, social bridge evenings can be relaxed and entertaining or sheer, unadulterated hell. Here, to increase the likelihood of your experience being a consistently good one, is a run-down of vital information:

- If you are hosting the evening yourself, accept that your bridge will suffer as you worry about temperature, drinks, food, etc. **Go easy on yourself** too; it's not really catastrophic if you find yourself with only seven people, the dog has eaten the red deck of cards, and the oven knob comes off in your hand …

- **Avoid bridge at Christmas**, or on other family occasions. A distant relative of mine, a bridge author in the 1930s, played bridge on his honeymoon, and seemed genuinely shocked when his wife had other plans.

- If you must play family bridge, and you cut for partners and end up with adolescents, former husbands or mothers-in-law, **ensure a ready supply of drink or drugs** – it's the only way to turn their tactless, insulting and provocative comments into innocuous *bon mots* …

- **Don't let husbands and wives play together**. Many bridge teachers require a marriage guidance diploma, and regular sessions in a floatation tank, to survive classes of married couples. Let the boys take on the girls for some healthy rivalry.

- **Play for decent stakes**. Playing for matchsticks, Maltesers or the washing-up just encourages people to get bored, and start sticking in erroneous overcalls and ridiculous sacrifices. The purpose of the stake is not gambling; it is a natural control mechanism to improve the game. (Mind you, when I used to play a boys versus girls game on a Friday evening, we always played for the washing-up, and my hands saw the insides of rubber gloves weekly.)

- **Hit the deck.** Shuffle the cards well; you cannot shuffle too much. The old wives' tale of shuffling the spots off the cards is just that – a tale.
  You benefit when the cards are properly randomised: correct techniques, accurate play, good bidding will all work in your favour. If you riffle-shuffle, seven times should be your minimum. If your splat them about, carry on shuffling, at least, until partner finishes dealing.

Shuffle well when dealing boards for Pairs or Teams games; the less you shuffle, the more likely the hands will be balanced – making the whole game less exciting.

An American friend and I played partnership Chicago in a club in North Hollywood a few years ago. We were invited to the big table to play against two seemingly friendly men. Our opponents, who played well, starting taking some very peculiar lines of play – against the odds – and found them working each time. I watched them dealing and suddenly it became clear. The dealer was distributing the cards widely, flicking each one up as he did so. His partner could see every card. For an opponent to know the position of the cards every other deal is a big advantage.

I told the dealer I could see the cards he dealt and didn't want to take advantage of this. He went a deep plum colour. As he dealt again, angling the cards slightly away from me, but still opening them to his opposite number, my partner commented that he too could see the cards – at which the dealer turned puce. After that, the cards were dealt properly. Later, I discovered my canny partner had suspected cheating also.

At the time, I felt quite clever to spot this and, as we came away a few dollars up, it had all been quite exciting – but I think it was depressing: cheating is much less fun than playing bridge.

- Finally, a tip more valuable to you than any other. Quite seriously, it will win you points, money, and satisfaction. Follow the guidance given to me by a charming elderly French lady many years ago. She used to say, **'Cherish your partner.'** And she was right. If you can crack a smile from time to time, you'll find everyone has a much better evening …

TOP TIPS QUIZ

Test yourself with these questions. If you're not sure of the answer, or if you get it wrong, refer immediately to the indicated tip. This way, you'll improve your game permanently. Turn to page 192 for the answers.

1) What would you open on each of these hands?

a	b	c	d
♠ 76	♠ KJ6	♠ Q	♠ 97
♥ A85	♥ AQ	♥ KJ63	♥ Q6
♦ 2	♦ AQ98	♦ A642	♦ AKQJ1086
♣ KQJ8763	♣ 5432	♣ Q973	♣ J8

2) Partner opens 1S. What do you respond on each of these hands?

a	b	c	d
♠ 975432	♠ 742	♠ Q985	♠ J753
♥ 8	♥ 63	♥ A2	♥ AQ7
♦ A964	♦ KJ86	♦ KQJ6	♦ 5
♣ 75	♣ QJ42	♣ Q84	♣ AJ843

3) Partner opens 1D. What do you respond?

a	b	c	d
♠ J85	♠ Q864	♠ AQJ6	♠ QJ9
♥ Q65	♥ 82	♥ 7532	♥ KJ5
♦ 2	♦ 54	♦ K4	♦ QJ87
♣ KJ9864	♣ AQJ32	♣ A32	♣ A98

4) Your RHO opens 1NT (12–14); he is vulnerable. What action do you take?

a	b	c	d
♠ AQ3	♠ 52	♠ AKQJ87	♠ Q105
♥ J6	♥ QJ9854	♥ 63	♥ K65
♦ A2	♦ AJ10	♦ Q42	♦ AKJ
♣ KQJ976	♣ 32	♣ 95	♣ Q532

5) Partner opens 1H; you reply 1S; he re-bids 2C. What do you bid now?

a	*b*	*c*	*d*
♠ AJ86	♠ AJ10864	♠ AQJ87	♠ QJ987
♥ J6	♥ 2	♥ K6	♥ -
♦ AQ92	♦ J54	♦ K42	♦ AKQJ8
♣ Q75	♣ K32	♣ J53	♣ KJ4

6) Your opponents bid 1NT-3NT. What do you lead?

a	*b*	*c*	*d*
♠ 93	♠ KQJ32	♠ J5	♠ 64
♥ A42	♥ 2	♥ 9853	♥ 98742
♦ QJ96	♦ A75	♦ 743	♦ AQJ
♣ KJ73	♣ 8763	♣ 9853	♣ Q102

7) You are in 3NT; your RHO leads 5♥ and East plays J♥. You win with K♥. Which opponent must you not permit to gain the lead: East or West?

	♥ 96	
5♥ led		J♥ played
	♥ KQ2	

8) You are in 3NT, and you have to play this suit to try to make three tricks. What should you do?

♥ AK63

♥ J72

9) Your LHO opens 1D; partner passes, and RHO responds 1S. What do you bid?

♠ 72
♥ AQ864
♦ K32
♣ A87

10) Your LHO opens 1D; partner doubles; RHO passes. What do you bid?

a	b	c	d
♠ A3	♠ 832	♠ KJ85	♠ 64
♥ Q9642	♥ 6432	♥ KJ94	♥ 98
♦ 632	♦ 875	♦ 743	♦ AQ8
♣ AK7	♣ 942	♣ AJ	♣ AQ7432

11) Your LHO opens 1C; partner overcalls 1S; RHO passes. What do you bid?

a	b	c	d
♠ 93	♠ QJ32	♠ K85	♠ J97532
♥ AQ32	♥ 2	♥ A87	♥ 7
♦ A532	♦ A7532	♦ KQJ5	♦ A65
♣ Q73	♣ 876	♣ 532	♣ 843

12) Against 4S, West leads Q♣. How many losers have you? What is your basic plan?

♠ Q83
♥ Q865
♦ 84
♣ K73

♠ AKJ75
♥ 74
♦ AK6
♣ A82

13) At Love All, partner opens 1S; RHO doubles. What do you bid?

a	b	c	d
♠ K742	♠ KJ97	♠ KJ85	♠ Q5
♥ 62	♥ 62	♥ A2	♥ QJ98
♦ 753	♦ QJ87	♦ 743	♦ Q86
♣ 8642	♣ J94	♣ A962	♣ Q985

14) Partner opens 1NT. What do you respond?

a	b	c	d
♠ AQ86	♠ 86542	♠ KJ85	♠ 643
♥ AJ74	♥ QJ96	♥ KJ94	♥ 98
♦ K832	♦ 8752	♦ 743	♦ 4
♣ 7	♣ –	♣ Q2	♣ AQJ7432

15) Assuming that partner does not support you, what are your first three bids on this hand?

♠ 6
♥ AKQ95
♦ KQJ874
♣ 2

16) You are in 3NT; West leads 4♦. What is your basic plan? When East plays 10♦, with which card do you win the trick?

♠ 83
♥ 65
♦ K53
♣ KQJ1073

♠ A94
♥ AK872
♦ AJ
♣ 82

17) What do you open with these hands?

a	b	c	d
♠ A7	♠ AQ	♠ Q107	♠ AKQ9643
♥ AJ74	♥ AQ	♥ K6	♥ J7
♦ Q9832	♦ J752	♦ Q109	♦ 432
♣ 54	♣ J6432	♣ A10985	♣ 9

18) You open 1H; partner responds 3H. What is your next bid?

a	b	c	d
♠ AQ5	♠ A6	♠ A65	♠ 5
♥ AJ94	♥ AQ8632	♥ AQJ983	♥ K76432
♦ Q98	♦ 8	♦ KQJ7	♦ A2
♣ KJ9	♣ J754	♣ –	♣ KQJ4

19) Your opponents bid 1H-3H-4H. What do you lead from these hands?

a	b	c	d
♠ 84	♠ 8653	♠ J10865	♠ A752
♥ J74	♥ 964	♥ AJ97	♥ 642
♦ QJ108	♦ 2	♦ Q109	♦ A85
♣ A964	♣ KJ432	♣ 8	♣ A103

20) You are in 6H; West leads K♦. What is your basic plan?

♠ J642
♥ QJ95
♦ AJ
♣ K86

♠ AQ9
♥ AK8742
♦ 8
♣ AQ7

QUIZ ANSWERS

If you get the answer wrong, go immediately to the tip shown

1   a) 1C – Tip 23   b) 1C – Tip 10   c) Pass – Tip 8   d) 3NT – Tip 29

2   a) 4S – Tip 2   b) 2S – Tip 37   c) 3NT – Tip 102   d) 4D – Tip 103

3   a) 1NT – Tip 3   b) 1S – Tip 44   c) 1H – Tip 45   d) 3NT – Tip 102

4   a) Dbl – Tip 18   b) 2H – Tip 19   c) Pass – Tip 19   d) Pass – Tip 18

5   a) 3NT – Tip 3   b) 2S – Tip 104   c) 2D – Tip 30   d) 3NT – Tip 5

6   a) Q♦ – Tip72   b) K♠ – Tip 72   c) J♠ – Tip 74   d) 9♥ – Tip 73

7   East – Tip 57

8   Lead low towards your J♥ – Tip 72

9   Pass – really important – Tip 105

10   a) 4H – Tip 43   b) 1H – Tip 43   c) 2D – Tip 42   d) 3NT – Tip 43

11   a) Pass – Tip 27   b) 3S – Tip 27   c) 2C – Tip 42   d) 4S – Tip 27

12   You have four losers: ♥74, your third club, and 6♦. Your basic plan is to ruff 6♦ in dummy before drawing trumps – Tip 66

13   a) 2S – Tip 38   b) 3S – Tip 38   c) 2NT – Tip 38   d) 1NT – Tip 38

14   a) 2C – Tip 13   b) 2C – Tip 14   c) Pass – Tip 14   d) 2C – Tip 14

15   1D, then hearts, then hearts again – to show 6–5 distribution – Tip 49

16   Your basic plan is to establish dummy's clubs. However, because the opponents will hold-up their Ac, you must retain an outside entry. For that reason, you must win trick one with Ad, so that, having pushed out Ac, you can return to dummy by playing Jd to Kd – Tip 62

17 a) Pass – Tip 113 b) 1NT – Tip 114 c) 1NT – Tip 12 d) 1S – Tip 113

18 a) 3NT – Tip 95 b) 4H – Tip 108 c) 3S – Tip 20 d) 4NT – Tip 21

19 a) Q♦ – Tip 94 b) 2♦ – Tip 94 c) J♠ – Tip 90 d) 2♥ – Tip 88

20 You have a certain loser in spades and a finesse to take. You want to avoid having to finesse, instead forcing West to lead a spade to you. To achieve this, win trick 1 with A♦, draw trumps, and play out all your clubs, finishing in dummy. Now, lead J♦ and pitch 9♠ from hand. West, who is marked with Q♦, must win, and is endplayed – Tip 68.

ABOUT THE AUTHOR

Paul Mendelson is best known as the *Financial Times*'s bridge correspondent and as a leading author on bridge and poker. He won the National Schools' Championship in 1983 and has continued to win county and national events ever since. He is the author of six books on bridge, three on poker and one on the analysis of casino games. Paul has lectured on bridge throughout the UK, and also in the USA, Australia, Spain, Portugal and South Africa. He administrated the world-renowned International Pairs tournament for seven years and is known to many of the world's finest players.

Paul believes that enjoying the game and being determined to win are not mutually exclusive, and it is his laughter you hear at many a bridge event.